PENGUIN BOOKS

THE FEMALE DIGITAL REVOLUTION

Nimisha Tailor is a competition and regulation specialist with international experience. She has advised large tech companies, central banks, think tanks and international organizations in the areas of digital finance, digital trade, data governance, e-commerce, and logistics. She has worked on consulting projects in Asia Pacific, the US, and Latin America and brings a gender lens to digital policies and regulations. Previously, she was deputy director at the Competition and Consumer Commission of Singapore and has worked at competition authorities in the UK, New Zealand, and Australia (secondment).

Nimisha is passionate about developing the next generation of leaders and mentors, young female professionals and university students, globally and regionally. As a mentor for the NexGen Keynote Women Speakers programme, she has supported talented women to make impactful speeches on stage by drawing on her public and private sector work experience.

Nimisha served in the UK Government Economic Service and has a MSc degree in Economics from the London School of Economics and Political Science.

ADVANCE PRAISE FOR
THE FEMALE DIGITAL REVOLUTION

'The Female Digital Revolution is a compelling call to action, illuminating the transformative power of technology in reshaping the role of women in our digital era. With the warmth of storytelling and the depth of research, Nimisha Tailor invites us to dance with possibility, urging us to embrace the digital era's transformative power and ensure no woman is left behind in the rhythm of progress.'

—Wida Schmidt, CEO, Carrier Community (Germany)

'Nimisha Tailor provides a compelling argument for why investors should champion female tech founders—for the benefit of us all. *The Female Digital Revolution* is a must-read for anyone looking to make impactful investments in technology.'

—Tim Deeson, founder, IfWeRaise, board advisor, Angel Investor (UK)

'Simple yet insightful case for how technology can further accelerate societal progress through more participation from women.'

—Ray Wong, former senior director, LinkedIn APAC Marketing (Singapore)

'Nimisha Tailor's *The Female Digital Revolution* is a timely book with inspiring stories of incredible women who are innovators and leaders in the technology world. I'm so glad that Tailor puts a spotlight on the impact of women in the data center industry in this book. Women are playing an indispensable role in building this critical digital infrastructure, which is the foundation for so much of the technology we use in every aspect of our lives.'

—Nancy Novak, chief innovation officer, Compass Datacenters (US)

'*The Female Digital Revolution* showcases how women are disrupting the gatekeepers of technology. Women deserve the right to understand and participate in digital spaces as much as they want, and reading this book is a great way to start.'

—Aleisha Amohia, technical lead,
Catalyst (New Zealand)

'Nimisha has expertly crafted a captivating book that is essential for aspiring entrepreneurs and women seeking growth and success within the digital space. It serves as a valuable guide for companies and governments aiming to bolster female entrepreneurship and support their advancement in the digital economy.'

—Eleanor A. Sarpong, senior digital development
consultant, board director Delwik Group,
UN Women UK Delegate (UK)

'An engaging book that pushes the skill relevance, women empowerment and level playing field narrative to the front row, while encouraging male leaders to step up their sponsorship and advocacy.'

—Tarun Kumar Kalra, VP, head of sales APAC,
Apptio, an IBM Company (Singapore)

'This book covers the most important technology topics and the benefits it can have for women. Written by my friend Nimisha Tailor who has been an expert in her field for a very long time.'

—Elly de Vrijer, partner & practice leader, Women
in Tech, Hightech Partners (Austria)

The Female Digital Revolution

Nimisha Tailor

PENGUIN BOOKS

An imprint of Penguin Random House

PENGUIN BOOKS

Penguin Books is an imprint of the Penguin Random House group of companies
whose addresses can be found at global.penguinrandomhouse.com

Published by Penguin Random House SEA Pte Ltd
40 Penjuru Lane, #03-12, Block 2
Singapore 609216

Penguin
Random House
SEA

First published in Penguin Books by Penguin Random House SEA 2024

ISBN 9789815144888

Typeset in Garamond by MAP Systems, Bengaluru, India

www.penguin.sg

*For my mum, who enrolled in a computing class
so she could send me an email to say 'hello'*

Author's Note

My parent's shop in Luton, England is where I spent most of my school holidays, meeting different customers like office workers buying newspapers and kids buying sweets. Years later, the area around the shop became flooded with university students living in nearby accommodation. Our customers changed and we stocked less magazines and more grocery items. Today, with economic and technological changes, many shops operate online, stocking large varieties of goods that anyone can buy on their smartphones.

Throughout my career, moving continents, I've met many women who skilfully adapt to change. I was impressed with how these fearless women leveraged economic and technological changes to forge careers that better serve their mission, skills, or personal lives. But I also met talented women who had little knowledge of the extent of digitalization occurring in our economy or were unclear on how it relates to them. On the other hand, I noticed some men operate in their own circles, focusing on not just 'cutting edge' but what was described as 'bleeding edge' technology. Yet as a consultant, I found governments and international organizations pushing for inclusive digital policies. I couldn't help thinking that there was a disconnect. I was curious. I interviewed a number of experts and professionals in the technology sector, from different cultures and countries, to understand their perspectives.

The common theme was the need for **awareness, support, and inspiration**. To fill this gap, I wrote this book with four objectives in mind. The first is to celebrate the brilliant women who have shattered stereotypes and pushed boundaries using digital technology. From startups to multinational corporations, from policy advocacy to groundbreaking innovations, these women have left an indelible mark on our economies and societies. Yet we don't talk about them enough. Second, is for the book to appeal to a wide audience. I want to raise awareness and motivate action through simple stories and examples. I also want men to be part of the conversation and consider the role they play. Third, the book is for an international audience with global examples, as well as local examples from towns, villages, and smart cities. Digital technology spans across different countries, in different stages of technological development. There is just as much to learn from developing economies as there is from developed economies. Fourth, the book is for women and girls from all backgrounds. All females are not the same and many have different interests. This book delves into the experiences, challenges, and triumphs of different women who have navigated the complex landscape of technology, from coding to digital leadership roles and everything in between. Enjoy reading.

Foreword

by Dame Paula Rebstock

I was described as fearless, confrontational, and controversial. As a leader, you cannot let criticism distract you. It's important to lead with purpose and have support around you. This is what makes women's leadership different to men. Women are drawn to mission and purpose and their representation in our economies is vital, especially as economies digitally transform. *The Female Digital Revolution* teaches us how women can and are using technology as a key enabler for driving their mission, whether it be in business, in government, in our communities, or within our homes. Women are using smartphones, digital platforms, and digital payments to change their lives for the better. But change requires you to be bold and to overcome challenges.

I have been honoured to be recognized for my public service. In the 2009 Queen's Birthday Honours, I was appointed a Companion of the New Zealand Order of Merit for public services and in 2016, I was promoted to Dame Companion of the same order. As a bold leader, I've made difficult decisions to drive change for the greater good. Through the women's network Onbeingbold, which is a collaboration of business leaders in New Zealand, I have shared my experience to inspire women at all stages of their experience. I see many women facing challenges. Whether it's progressing their careers, managing work life balance or setbacks in personal and professional goals. The key is to turn these challenges into opportunities. *The Female Digital Revolution* eloquently puts the spotlight on these evolving challenges in our digital world and tells us how to turn them into fulfilling lives for women and take advantage of the untapped opportunities.

I first met Nimisha in the boardroom. At that time, I was chair of the New Zealand Commerce Commission and was responsible for making markets competitive. I needed to make a bold decision. I listened to Nimisha present her research, analysis, and recommendations. Her job was not for the faint hearted. Often the issues were complex, or the companies being investigated were high profile. She needed to absorb a vast amount of information, keep a critical eye, and communicate in a compelling manner. Nimisha continues to display these strengths in this insightful book. Nimisha, a fellow alumnus from the London School of Economics and Political Science, has skilfully taken her international experience as an economist, consultant, entrepreneur, skill-based volunteer, mentor, and mentee to encourage women to consider careers in the digital economy and to innovate for women. She has taken her personal insights, stories of men and women from around the globe and combined them with research to provide a powerful roadmap for men and women, government, businesses, and investors in how they can support women in their digital endeavours.

Serving on different boards for companies involved in electricity, transport, health, insurance, and New Zealand's Stock Exchange, I believe more and more businesses will need to lead with mission, creating more demand for female representation. Women are bringing new ways of working and engaging technology to bring real value to companies, boards, and government. *The Female Digital Revolution* highlights the different ways in which women are showing up in our organizations, leading a technological revolution, as well as their own revolution.

We all need to be challenged in our thinking, whether we are in government, in business, or the social sector, and this book provides actionable advice to different economic agents so that they can be catalysts of change in their jurisdiction. I found this book to be informative and inspirational, motivating women young and old to understand different digital technologies, the career paths available, and the digital skills they need. This book can help women to be bold. It can also help men and women support women on being bold.

Introduction

'None of us present today have accomplished anything by ourselves,' said Taylor Swift when she received an honorary doctorate from New York University in 2022. The thirtysomething was awarded the degree for her remarkable achievements in the music industry. She is the first woman to have won three Grammy awards—Album of the Year once and Billboard's Woman of the Decade Award twice. Her songs are well known and relatable to the billions of fans she has all over the world.

Even more intriguing, is that the talented singer-songwriter has a significant digital presence. You can access her music by downloading digital albums and watch her music videos through streaming sites. You can purchase branded merchandise and online tickets to attend her concerts, and you can also chat with her online on various platforms like Tumblr, Twitter, and Instagram. Through social media, she has built a strong online community, where fans can engage in all things Swift. She has billions of online followers and actively interacts with her fans on social media, responding to messages, and commenting and liking posts, making fans feel like a part of her world. One fan created an online game called Swiftball, a Taylor-fied fantasy football game started by a Twitter user, in which fans attempt to predict outfits and surprise songs for her concert.

Swift is a great example of how someone can leverage digital technology, and the spending power of women. She has masterfully generated online content and adapted it to different online channels. She is known for leaving a continuous trail of Easter eggs for her fans to find as clues for her next song. Her successful marketing strategy is being used as a case study for teaching digital marketing. Why? Because she is making smart business decisions. Economic professors are calling it 'Swifteconomics'—rightly so, as she is the second richest woman in the US and is playing a significant part in boosting the US economy.

On average, almost 54,000 fans attended each of her Eras Tour concerts in the US. Each American show grossed around $13 million, bringing Swift more than $300 million after playing the first twenty-two concerts.[1] When concert tickets for the tour went on sale, the online ticketing platform struggled to manage the tsunami of fans looking to buy tickets. Approximately 14 million users logged into the Ticketmaster site during the 'verified fan' presale on 15 November, resulting in the sale of 2.4 million presale tickets. It is estimated that the Eras tour could generate up to $4.6 billion in consumer spending for the US economy in total.[2] The tour has boosted tourism with increased online spending on hotels, flights, and new outfits to wear to the concert. The Federal Reserve Bank of Philadelphia stated that Swift's tour stimulated travel and tourism in the region, making May the strongest month

---

[1] Alëna Kuzub. '"Swiftonomics", or the smart business choices Taylor Swift makes that affect the U.S. economy.' *Northeastern Global News*. August 2023. https://news.northeastern.edu/2023/08/11/taylor-swift-economy-impact/
Elizabeth Faragi and Katie Walsh. '"Swiftonomics": How Taylor Swift has impacted the economy.' *Hi's eye*. October 2023. https://hiseye.org/10825/his-eye/swiftonomics-how-taylor-swift-has-impacted-the-economy/
[2] 'The Taylor Swift Impact – 5 Months and $5+ Billion.' *US Travel Association*. September 2023. https://www.ustravel.org/news/taylor-swift-impact-5-months-and-5-billion

for hotel revenue in the city since the pandemic.[3] In Las Vegas, it was Swift's presence, not gambling, that caused the highest post-pandemic tourism spending.

Swift's influence extends well beyond her singing. She is a role model inspiring girls and women to create their own future. She has spoken out on gender differences in the music industry, encouraged people to vote in the elections, and used her song lyrics to bring awareness on social issues. Even academics have taken an interest in her extraordinary influence. In 2024, six universities across Australia and New Zealand came together to host a 'Swiftposium', namely an academic conference.[4] The event coincided with the Swift Eras tour in Australia and involved discussion of 'Swift's popularity and its profound implications for a range of issues including gender, popular culture, literature, the economy, and the music industry'.[5]

Digital Empowerment

Taylor Swift is not the only woman making her mark using digital technology to empower herself and millions of others. Despite the tech industry being dominated by a male workforce, a rising wave of successful women are reshaping the sector and many others. Some of these women are like Swift and are extraordinary. Powerful global women are advocating for diversity and inclusion in technology and other related sectors, recognizing the importance of equal representation and opportunities.

---

[3] Zahra Tayeb. 'Hollywood is helping boost the economy as fans flock to "Barbie", "Oppenheimer", and Taylor Swift's Eras Tour.' *Business Insider.* August 2023. https://www.businessinsider.in/policy/economy/news/hollywood-is-helping-boost-the-economy-as-fans-flock-to-barbie-oppenheimer-and-taylor-swifts-eras-tour/articleshow/102449620.cms

[4] https://swiftposium2024.com/

[5] https://swiftposium2024.com/

For example, Dr Fei-Fei Li—a renowned researcher of artificial intelligence (AI) and professor at Stanford University—has made visionary contributions to AI but also actively works to increase diversity and inclusion in the field. Melinda Gates, who is philanthropist and global advocate for women and girls, is on a mission to reduce the gender gap in digital connectivity so women and girls can participate more fully in the digital economy. Amy Hood is the first female chief financial officer in Microsoft and now works to increase the company's long-term growth while promoting a culture of equality.[6] Hood is focused on bringing additional Black-owned partners and suppliers into Microsoft's network. She is a big supporter of equality for women in senior leadership roles and speaks regularly at events such as Fortune's Most Powerful Women Summit.

On the other hand, many, many of the women using technology or working in the technology sector are ordinary women. Both types are making significant contributions to the economy. On a national and local level, women are establishing digital businesses, startups, and online ventures, driving innovation and economic growth in sectors like e-commerce, digital health, finance, and education. Digital platforms like Etsy, Amazon, and Shopify allow women to sell their products and services online, while tools like Squarespace and Wix make it easy to create a website or blog to promote their brand. More women are acquiring digital skills, from coding and programming to data analysis and digital marketing. Women are accessing online education and digital learning platforms, allowing them to acquire knowledge and skills in a wide range of fields including science, technology, engineering, and mathematics (STEM). Women are taking on leadership roles in technology companies, influencing digital

---

[6] Amanda Stevens and Amanda Hetler. 'Top 9 most influential women in technology'. *TechTarget*. March 2023. https://www.techtarget.com/whatis/feature/Top-9-most-influential-women-in-technology

strategy, and playing crucial roles in technological development and innovation.

Women are using digital platforms and mobile apps to manage their health and wellness, from fitness tracking to telemedicine and mental health support. They are creating digital content on social media, podcasts, and blog platforms like YouTube, using these outlets to inform, entertain, and engage audiences on a wide range of topics. Women are also advocating for women's rights, gender equality, and other societal issues through online platforms.

We are seeing a female digital revolution, characterized by women's active engagement with digital tools, platforms, and opportunities, leading to personal as well as public change. This movement has the potential to advance gender equality in the digital age. But there are challenges. While women are benefitting from the current industrial revolution, there is scope for more women to be involved in it and benefit from it. In 2021, mobile technologies and services generated $4.5 trillion of economic value added, or 5 per cent of gross domestic product (GDP) globally, but women in both developing and developed countries who are unable to connect to or use mobile technologies risk being left behind.

A key concern is that not enough innovative technologies are being developed *by women* or *for women*, leading to missed opportunities for businesses and governments to cater to female needs. More representation, particularly in managerial roles is needed to influence the design and policies for digital technologies.[7] When women represent more than 20 per cent of a company's management team, research shows that companies have approximately 10 per cent higher innovation revenues.[8]

---

[7] 'Women in the Digital Economy Fund'. *USAID*. April 2023. https://www.usaid.gov/digital-development/gender-digital

[8] 'Boosting Women in Technology in Southeast Asia'. *Boston Consulting Group*. *October* 2020. https://www.bcg.com/publications/2020/boosting-women-in-southeast-asia-tech-sector

There is also an urgent need to train and upskill women and increase their basic digital literacy to enable them to engage with and participate in the digital economy. As you will learn in this book, greater inclusivity can keep women in technology-related roles and overcome talent shortages.[9]

While women in STEM continue to be essential, we also need women from other professions like lawyers, accountants, statisticians, and marketing and human resource professionals to drive the digital transformation taking place in businesses—in both the government and in the social sector. We need, not just more women in technical roles like software engineers and cloud computing, but also in digital leadership roles to drive digital transformation, particularly in growing industries like e-commerce, health, and finance. Digital leadership is the ability to utilize digital technology like AI, cloud computing and blockchain effectively in problem-solving, decision-making, and management. This mindset shift from '*women in tech*' to '*women in the digital economy*' has the scope to open more doors for women by taking advantage of their changing role in the fourth industrial revolution. In launching the Women in Digital Economy Fund, Kamala Harris, vice president of the US, described digital technologies to be 'great equalizers in terms of giving those who have access equal opportunity and availability to information, to education, to networks in a way that improves and empowers themselves, their families, their community, and all of society benefits'.[10]

The Female Digital Revolution thus takes you on a journey of women in the digital economy. It starts by explaining two key drivers of change transforming our societies and economies. The

---

[9] 'Resetting Tech Culture'. *Accenture* and *Girls Who Code*.

[10] 'Remarks by Vice President Harris in Meeting with Private Sector and Philanthropic Leaders on Digital Inclusion in Africa'. *The White House*. April 2023. https://www.whitehouse.gov/briefing-room/speeches-remarks/2023/04/01/remarks-by-vice-president-harris-in-meeting-with-private-sector-and-philanthropic-leaders-on-digital-inclusion-in-africa/

first is the digital revolution, that is, the growing digitalization of our economy. It is so significant and widespread that it is more appropriate to consider it as the 'digital economy'. Second is the female revolution, namely, the changing role of women during the decades of industrial revolution and how their personal and professional lives have changed. Combing these influential trends presents the current digital landscape of how women are using digital devices or mobile apps for safer, healthier, and more entertaining lives. These range from digital tools like business software or Google Workspace for remote and flexible working, mobile apps for tracking fertility and pregnancy, to e-sports as a new profession for women and young girls.

The second chapter takes a deep dive into the different types of digital technologies currently being deployed as well as future technology like quantum computing. We explain what the technology is, how it is used, and how women are benefitting from it or being impacted by it. The chapter showcases digital equipment like drones and quantum computing, to frameworks like digital identities used to make payments or travel, or software tools such as AI and platforms like the metaverse that bring arts and culture to life. It provides a backdrop to the future potential of the female digital economy. Despite the significant benefits digital technologies are delivering for women, there are still significant untapped opportunities. For instance, within the e-commerce sector, which is just one aspect of the digital economy, women could add over $300 billion in Africa and Southeast Asia between 2025 and 2030. In chapter three, we discuss the different types of missed opportunities within an economic context, highlighting risks of no action, such as biased algorithms, unequal access, cyberbullying, or products that just don't meet women's needs. All of which could force women to distance themselves. There is a missed opportunity to make digital technologies inclusive to create more rewarding careers and better pay for women in the digital economy—better innovation *for women by women*, better investor returns from women-owned or -led businesses, and better policies and regulations to protect women from online harm.

The question is, how do you seize these opportunities? Who is responsible? In chapter four, we invite you to start thinking of women as powerful digital economic agents shaping our economy and implementing targeted initiatives. We provide examples from China, the US, Latin America, Europe, the Middle East, and Africa to show women's role as digital consumers, digital creators, digital entrepreneurs, digital business owners or leaders, and as digital government. We share stories about women leading the largest digital bank in Latin America, the female entrepreneurs in Indonesia (*warungs*), the woman transforming Barcelona into a smart city, and the woman driving digital government in the UAE.

In chapter five, we take a look at what it's like to be a fintech startup, climate tech activist, AI doctor, datacentre designer, digital artist, cybersecurity specialist, data manager, and data privacy specialists. By sharing the career paths of women, the hope is that other women and young girls can see how they themselves can be part of the digital economy—in whatever way they want—as virtually every industry is being digitalized to some extent. This is not just about developing technical skills, although this will be essential for jobs like software engineering and cloud computing, but also about the importance of digital leadership and entrepreneurship. Whether you are a lawyer, nurse, accountant, administrative assistant or civil servant, you will need to learn how to use digital devices, platforms and software, which are changing how companies and organizations function and perform. We talk about the digital skills needed in chapter six and draw on examples from India, Southeast Asia, and New Zealand to learn how they are training young girls and women and supporting a female tech workforce.

While women must invest in themselves, they cannot do it alone. There must be support. There must be support from men but in a way that also respects and recognizes their changing roles in our economy and society. Chapter seven discusses the role of men in the female digital revolution, and chapter eight provides guidance on how companies, investors, and government leaders can provide tailored support and be active participants and contributors to the female digital revolution.

Chapter 1

The (Female) Digital Economy

'Womenomics offers a solution with its core tenet that a country that hires and promotes more women grows economically, and no less importantly, demographically as well.'[1]

—Shinzo Abe, former prime minister of Japan

When former Japanese Prime Minister Shinzo Abe, addressed the World Assembly for Women in Tokyo, in 2015, he said that Abenomics was 'Womenomics'.[2] The prime minister was being praised for introducing government policies to increase the number of women in work. In the 1990s, not enough women were working in Japan. The country had one of the lowest labour participation rates for women in the developed world.[3] In 2012, recognizing the power of women's economic participation,

---

[1] Shinzo Abe. 'Unleashing the Power of Womenomics'. *Wall Street Journal.* September 2013. https://www.wsj.com/articles/shinzo-abe-unleashing-the-power-of-8216womenomics8217-1380149475

[2] 'Opening Speech by Prime Minister Shinzo Abe at the Open Forum, World Assembly for Women in Tokyo: WAW! 2015'. August 2015. https://www.mofa.go.jp/files/000096924.pdf

[3] 'Japan introduces "womenomics" to counter the country's aging workforce and boost GDP'. *Council on Foreign Relations.* https://www.cfr.org/womens-participation-in-global-economy/case-studies/japan/

Prime Minister Abe adopted 'Womenomics'—a concept introduced by Kathy Matsui chief Japan strategist for Goldman Sachs. In 1999, Matsui, published a report highlighting that female consumption was an important source of strength in the struggling Japanese economy.[4] Her report listed sixteen Japanese companies that were either poised to benefit from female consumption or were proactive in employing women. Matsui argued that an increase in Japan's female labour participation rate from the prevailing rate of 50 per cent to 59 per cent could boost the country's real GDP growth in 2000–2010 to 2.5 per cent per annum from 2.2 per cent. The Japanese government listened and introduced legislation to expand childcare, mandate equal pay for equal work, and tax reforms that gave women the incentive to work. The government also tried to increase the number of women in leadership positions, including cabinet roles in the government. While there is more work to be done, Japan now reports female labour participation that overtakes the US and Europe with generous parental leave benefits, improved gender transparency, and labour reforms.[5]

Prime Minister Abe was thinking of women within the broader economy and how he could maximize this underutilized resource. He recognized the economic benefits. This thinking can be extended within the context of technology. Just like women, technology is a source of economic growth. Combine them and economies can progress even further. For example, hiring more women in technology related industries can drive innovation, grow industries, create more jobs, and increase the standard of living for everyone. An international study found that gender diversity could contribute at least 20 per cent to a country's GDP

---

[4] '"Womenomics" Reveals the Power of the Purse in Japan'. *Goldman Sachs.* https://www.goldmansachs.com/our-firm/history/moments/1999-womenomics.html

[5] Kathy Matsui. 'Womenomics 5.0 Report. Goldman Sachs'. *Portfolio strategy research.* April 2019.

due to the different skill sets and strengths that women bring to the workforce.[6] Another study points out that the positive impact of diversity tends to be higher in knowledge intensive, high skilled, and innovation-driven sectors.[7]

To improve our understanding of the impact of women's access to and participation in the digital revolution, let's dive deep into two separate revolutions taking place. First is the technological revolution. Second is the female revolution. When you combine these powerful forces, we find that digital devices like smartphones and technologies like AI, Internet of Things (IoT), and blockchain are reshaping woman's lives, regardless of whether they live in urban cities or in remote regions of the world.

Technological Change

'A few years back, digitalisation was a topic for specialists. Now, it has become a topic for everyone, since digitalisation has impacted us all.'[8]

—Cécile Bernheim, president, S2E Partners.

The Austrian economist, Joseph Schumpeter, introduced the term 'creative destruction' in the 1940s to describe the way technological progress improves the lives of many, but only at the expense of a smaller few.[9] Technology reshapes work processes, production methods, and consumption patterns. Technology not only drives innovation and opportunities for growth, but it also presents challenges to traditional models of economic development.

---

[6] 'Transforming Corporate Culture to Advance All Women Equitably'. *Paradigm for Parity*.

[7] *All Hands In? Making Diversity Work for All*. OECD Publishing. 2020.

[8] Robert Mitson. 'Women in Digital: The obstacles and opportunities for an inclusive, digital world'. *Sherpany*.

[9] Joseph A. Schumpeter. *Capitalism, Socialism, and Democracy*. Harper and Brothers, New York.

Schumpeter's theory was 'out with the old and in with the new'. Producers and workers committed to older technology will be left stranded, while entrepreneurs and workers in new technologies will gain new profit opportunities.

During the industrial revolution, creative destruction was evident. The First Industrial Revolution in the 1700s transformed agricultural economies into large-scale manufacturing industries. Using coal and gas to produce steam power, the revolution introduced machines. The Second Industrial Revolution, which occurred between late 1800s and early 1900s, was a light bulb moment (literally). Electricity was invented and so was the telephone, the radio, and even the airplane. The way people worked and lived changed. People were able to move to different cities yet stay in touch with loved ones. This increased mobility and ability to communicate on the phone strengthened and by the late twentieth century, the Third Industrial Revolution, also known as the Digital Revolution, disrupted our lives by introducing computers. Not just desktop computers but also the minicomputers we now call smartphones. The digital revolution converted technology that was in an analogue format to a digital format. For example, CDs replaced analogue music such as vinyl records and cassette tapes. However, the digital revolution involved technology that operated in silos, and so a key theme of the Fourth Industrial Revolution—the one we are living through right now—is the interconnection of smart technologies. In 2016, Klaus Schwab, the World Economic Forum founder and economist first spoke about the speed, breadth, and depth of technological progress, labelling it the Fourth Industrial Revolution.[10] Klaus spoke of how all aspects of our economy—

---

[10] Klaus Schwab. 'The Fourth Industrial Revolution: what it means, how to respond'. *The World Economic Forum.* January 2016. https://www.weforum.org/agenda/2016/01/the-fourth-industrial-revolution-what-it-means-and-how-to-respond/

whether it was businesses, industries, or public services—were being digitalized. The Fourth Industrial Revolution describes our current world and how technologies like IoT, robotics, virtual reality (VR), and AI are changing our economies in significant ways.

Indeed, digitalization has disrupted traditional industries such as retail, banking, travel, entertainment, and transport. For example, even though you can physically go to the bank to make transactions, mobile banking on your smartphone is easier, faster, and more convenient, and is available 24/7. Similarly, online shopping helps people find and purchase many things, from toys and clothes to household essentials. This creative destruction continues, and it is no longer right to think of it as just a few key sectors becoming digitalized. With digital options everywhere our focus must now be on the 'digital economy'. The Organization for Economic Co-operation Development (OECD) defines the digital economy as 'all economic activity reliant on, or significantly enhanced by the use of digital inputs, including digital technologies, digital infrastructure, digital services and data'. It refers to all producers and consumers that are utilizing these digital inputs in their economic activities.[11]

The global digital economy makes up more than 15 per cent of the global GDP and the World Bank estimates it has grown 2.5 times faster over the previous ten years than the GDP of the physical world. Deemah Al Yahya, secretary-general of the Digital Cooperation Organization, expects the digital economy to contribute 30 per cent to the global GDP and create 30 million jobs by 2030.[12] The exponential rate of technological progress has already led to discussion on what the Fifth Industrial Revolution

---

[11] 'A roadmap toward a common framework for measuring the digital economy'. *OECD*. 2020.

[12] Arya Devi. 'DCO 2030: Digital economy to contribute 30% of global GDP and create 30 million jobs by 2030'. *Edge Middle East*. February 2023.

might look like. In this future world, it is envisaged that new technologies will facilitate humans collaborating with machines, namely 'Collaborative Robots' (known as Cobots). These robots would be equipped with ultrasonic sensors on robot arms that would detect the proximity of people, keeping them safe from colliding. The Sixth Industrial Revolution is expected to go even further and is understood to be where physical, digital, and biological worlds converge using advanced technologies such as quantum computing and nanotechnology.

Now that our focus is on the digital economy, with women making up half of the world's population, the question is what role are women playing in the digital economy? Let's explore how the role of women has changed during these decades of industrial revolution. How have their careers, education, and life choices changed? Understanding this history can shape future careers available for women in the digital economy.

The Changing Role of Women

'I grew up with a mother who said, "I'll arrange a marriage for you at eighteen," but she also said that we could achieve anything we put our minds to and encouraged us to dream of becoming prime minister or president.'

—Indra Nooyi, CEO, Pepsi

The industrial revolution is not the only revolution that has been taking place. Amidst these economic changes, the role of women has dramatically changed. As a result of the first and second industrial revolution, women entered the workforce to support their family as the men went to war. In Great Britian, women started working in textile mills and coal mines in large numbers. However, the working conditions were poor, leading to feminist movements to fight for workplace equality. Feminists continued to fight for equality, in particular, voting rights, as throughout the 1800s, women were denied the right to vote. By early 1900s, the suffragettes led the movement that gave women the right to vote, allowing them to change the direction of how the country was governed. The suffragettes also fought for equal access to education and employment, equality within marriage, and a married woman's right to her own property and wages.

To understand the changing role of women, we can draw insights from economic studies. For instance, Professor Claudia Goldin, an American Nobel Prize winner, studied the changing economic role of women in the US. Her research found that married women started to work less after the arrival of industrialization in the 1800s, but their employment picked up again in the 1900s as the service economy grew.[13] In her award-winning research 'The Quiet Revolution That Transformed Women's Employment, Education, and Family', just like the four industrial revolutions, she identified four distinct phases in the economic role of women.[14] She describes the first three as evolutionary and the final one as revolutionary, as women's aspirations changed from pursuing jobs to chasing careers. The first phase was that of the 'independent female worker', which referred to female workers in the US labour market from the late-nineteenth century to 1920s who were generally young, unmarried, and poorly educated. These young women were often either piece workers in manufacturing or worked as domestic helps and laundresses. The second phase was described as the easing of the 'constraints on married women's work'. Goldin found that from 1930 to 1950, participation rates for married women, aged

---

[13] Lucy Hooker. 'Nobel economics prize awarded to Claudia Goldin for work on women's pay'. *BBC News*. October 2023. https://www.bbc.com/news/business-67045408

[14] Claudia Goldin. 'The Quiet Revolution That Transformed Women's Employment, Education, and Family'. *AEA papers and proceedings*. Vol. 96 No. 2. May 2006.

thirty-five to forty-four years old, increased substantially. A key driver was the arrival of new information technologies, which meant that more office and clerical workers were required. There had also been an enormous growth in girls enrolling and graduating from high school from 1910 to 1930, leading to a large pool of skilled female workers. The third phase was what Goldin calls the 'roots of the revolution'. Married women continued to work, increasing women's labour participation in the US in the 1950s to 1970s. By the time we reached the fourth phase, 'the quiet revolution', women's expectation of the future had fundamentally changed. Women invested in education and sought careers, not jobs. Women got married later—they wanted to 'make a name' for themselves before having to choose to change their name.[15] Goldin finds this mindset change and the change in women's labour participation was supported by women gaining further control of their lives. Women now have more control over life decisions on when to get married and/or whether to have children as the introduction of the contraceptive pill gave them control of their reproductive rights and family planning.

Goldin's quiet revolution can be witnessed today in the midst of The Fourth Industrial Revolution. Women are creating their own identities and exercising choice. Some are choosing to be single, either by not marrying or getting divorced. Married women are having children later in life or not having them at all. Women are continuing to invest in education, empowering them to seek higher paying professions that provide financial independence. We see women of all ages making learning an important aspect of their lives. There are not just more girls going to school but there are also older women embarking on lifelong learning, to upskill

---

[15] Sarah Skwire. 'Claudia Goldin: A Personal Appreciation'. *EconLib*. October 2023 https://www.econlib.org/claudia-goldin-a-personal-appreciation/

and transition from old careers to new careers. There are now more women in leadership roles, including in politics, business, and academia. There has been a growing global movement to promote women's participation in decision-making. Research shows that companies with more than 30 per cent women executives were more likely to outperform those with fewer women executives, or none at all.[16] At the board level it is the same. In fact, a survey found that boards with fewer women were losing out.[17]

Women are making inroads into traditionally male-dominated fields, such as STEM. Research from the UK shows that the number of young women taking computer science degrees is growing faster than for any other British university subject.[18]

We see more women using the digital revolution to work, learn, play, connect, stay healthy, manage the home, save the planet, and be financially independent. As a result, key sectors like digital finance, digital health, and online education are rapidly growing with more consumers and companies and more products and services. This has a significant multiplier effect on the economy. It is worth noting that it's not that men aren't doing the same as women. The fact is they are adopting digital technologies into their homes and workplaces, albeit in a different way. One example is a study that shows that men are interacting in the metaverse less often than women.[19] We will learn more about the role of men

---

[16] Sundiatu Dixon-Fyle, Kevin Dolan, Dame Vivian Hunt, Sara Prince. 'Diversity wins: How inclusion matters'. *McKinsey & Company*. May 2021.

[17] 'Transforming Corporate Culture to Advance All Women Equitably'. *Paradigm for Parity*.

[18] 'Women choosing computing degrees in record numbers'. *BCS Chartered Institute for IT*. December 2022. https://www.bcs.org/articles-opinion-and-research/women-choosing-computing-degrees-in-record-numbers/

[19] Mina Alaghband and Lareina Yee. 'Even in the metaverse, women remain locked out of leadership roles'. *McKinsey & Company*. November 2022.

later, as this is also a key part of the female digital revolution. For now, our focus is on the current (and potentially future) way in which digitalization is impacting women.

Work

> 'We've noticed a growing trend of women leaving their traditional corporate tech jobs and embracing the freedom of freelancing. This is particularly beneficial for women living in remote areas and those returning to work after a break, as they can take advantage of the flexibility that freelancing offers.'[20]
>
> —Shilpa Jain, CEO, BeGig

As mentioned earlier, technological development has been driving decades of industrial revolutions. At the same time, digital devices and software are allowing women to change how they work, where they work, when they work, and for whom they work. Digital platforms, digital tools, and solutions have revamped women's world of work, accelerated by lockdowns during the pandemic. In the US, pre-pandemic, 26 per cent of women worked from home in 2019, which increased to 49 per cent in 2020 and fell to 41 per cent last year.[21] Remote working has helped women—especially mothers with young children—join or stay in the workforce. It has been described as a game changer in the US, where it is estimated

---

[20] Alka Jain. 'Breaking Barriers: How Technology is Empowering Women in the Workforce'. *Mint*. March 2023.

[21] Caitlin Gilbert, Teddy Amenabar, Hanna Zakharenko and Lindsey Bever. 'Remote work appears to be here to stay, especially for women'. *The Washington Post*. June 2023. https://www.washingtonpost.com/wellness/2023/06/22/remote-work-family-socialization-time-use/

that the labour force expanded by as much as 1.3 million women.[22] Having more women working is good for businesses and for the economy. Women bring unique perspectives, experiences, and skills to the table that can lead to new ideas and approaches. Companies that have an equal representation of women in the workforce tend to perform better.

Digital platforms like Upwork, Freelancer, Guru, and Fiverr make freelancing a viable option for women. These platforms allow freelancers to connect with potential clients for short-term jobs, and contracted work. The increased flexibility to manage their work and be their own boss allows more women to work, particularly if they are juggling family responsibilities at the same time. The Australian platform, Hire Her, is a Talent Marketplace for women and offers a diverse range of job types, including freelance, part-time, full-time, and project-based work. Its website states: 'We understand that women particularly parents have different needs and preferences when it comes to their careers, and we want to ensure that our platform caters to those needs.'[23]

Individuals who freelance through digital platforms are commonly described as workers in the gig economy, which is on the rise. In 2022, the global gig economy was valued at $413,930 million and is expected to reach $918,944 million by 2028.[24] Gig jobs provide women with an alternative work option, provided that the platform provides sufficient workers' rights and weeds out gender discrimination and biased behaviour online. With this in mind, Upwork has developed its own online community. The Upwork Women's Group hosts collaborative events, like a Safety

---

[22] Aki Ito. 'Remote work is having a huge and unexpected effect on women's careers'. *The Business Insider.* July 2023. https://www.businessinsider.in/policy/economy/news/the-pandemic-didnt-derail-womens-careers-it-supercharged-them-/articleshow/101666536.cms

[23] Hire Her website: https://gohireher.com/

[24] 'Gig Economy Market Size & Revenue by 2028'. *Global Newswire.*

Month Campaign and shares resources to improve cultural competency.[25]

In addition to platforms, digital tools allow for remote working, meaning that women can work from home instead of the office. Tools like video conferencing apps, cloud computing to store files, visual whiteboards, messaging and security apps are just some examples that have made remote working an everyday reality. This has made it easier for women to stay in professional jobs or set up their own side hustles. The pandemic has normalized the use of these tools, as most office workers were forced to work from home. During the pandemic, Zoom usage soared overnight. Since then, even more digital tools have been developed that improve productivity, project management, and management of remote teams.

Learn

'We are encouraged by how women are embracing online learning to develop new skills that can help accelerate their return to work and promote economic mobility.'[26]

—Jeff Maggioncalda, CEO, Coursera

Digitalization is also altering how women and young girls learn, giving them a chance to enhance their career opportunities and earning potential. Many economies have been able to transform by having women and girls stay in educational institutions for longer, and then join the workforce. Increased access to online learning has made this possible. Whether it be studying for undergraduate

---

[25] Upwork website: https://www.upwork.com/

[26] 'New Coursera Study Indicates a Narrowing Gender Gap in Online Learning'. *Business Wire*. September 2021. https://www.businesswire.com/news/home/20210909005279/en/New-Coursera-Study-Indicates-a-Narrowing-Gender-Gap-in-Online-Learning

or graduate level qualifications, or learning soft skills or hard skills, women are opting to learn through online education. It has opened significant doors for women, especially those with caregiving responsibilities who need to stay at home and for those who live remotely. International Finance Corporation research found that 45 per cent of women and 60 per cent of women caregivers in developing countries said they would have had to postpone or stop studies if online learning wasn't an option.[27]

In the past, online education acted as a career-training avenue for working mothers. However, now, online learning is enabling women to acquire new skills. During the pandemic, an online learning platform Coursera reported that women enrolled in courses at higher rates than before the pandemic. In 2019, women made up 47 per cent of learners. By 2021, this jumped to 52 per cent.[28] Furthermore, the research shows that women are learning better in online classrooms, as it is less intimidating. 'If they're in a classroom with male dominance, a lot of women won't even raise their hand.'[29] Online, women tend to be more engaged, posting on online forums and engaging with their instructors and peers. As a result, women are gaining skills for entry-level digital jobs, ranging from IT support and software development to user experience (UX) design and social media marketing. These skills are providing women with good careers in large technology firms like Google, IBM, Meta, and Salesforce to fill existing talent gaps.

With more women accessing and benefitting from online education, more providers are tailoring to their needs. Adult online learning is expected to more than double in value by 2026,

---

[27] 'Women and Online Learning in Emerging Markets'. *Coursera and European Commission*. July 2022.

[28] Adi Gaskell. 'Covid Saw a Boost In Online Learning Among Women'. *Forbes*. November 2021.

[29] 'Women Poised to Reap Benefits of Online Education'. *Best Colleges*. January 2022.

creating a $14 billion per annum revenue opportunity for online education providers.[30] There are also a large number of women setting up their own edutech firms. These firms provide access to online learning tools, for adults or children, which can be tailored to individual learning needs, across a vast range of topics and genres. One example is a digital library for kids. While working as a primary school teacher, Susie Seaton struggled to find decent classroom resources.[31] That motivated her to create a digital lesson library from her own spare bedroom. Her website Twinkl now has more than 625,000 resources. The company has over 710 members of staff and a business that operates in 200 countries around the world. Her website became popular for homeschooling during the pandemic as all the resources were free for parents and teachers across the globe. Seaton's idea shows how she leveraged on the wave of digitalization to bring educational resources to millions of children in the comfort of their home.

Play

'I wanted to revive the amateur tier of gamers, and give women gamers more chances to experience and realise their dreams of becoming an esports athlete.'[32]

—Tammy Tang, founder, Female Esports League

Tiffi is a little girl living in Candy Town. She loves sweets and, together with her friend Yeti, she sets out to explore the Candy Kingdom. This is the background to the popular mobile game

---

[30] 'Women and Online Learning in Emerging Markets'. Coursera and European Commission. July 2022.

[31] '5 women changing the face of EdTech'. *Hubbublabs*. https://hubbublabs. com/the-insider/5-women-changing-edtech/

[32] 'Game on: meet the ladies who levelled up for esports success'. *Kaya*. April 2022. https://www.mccy.gov.sg/KAYA/Youth/Game-On-meet-the-ladies-who-levelled-up-for-esports-success

Candy Crush. Within one year of its launch, Candy Crush became the most popular game on Facebook in 2013. What you may not realize is that the average Candy Crush player is female. She is thirty-five years old and plays, on average, for thirty-eight minutes a day.[33] Many of these female players are willing to pay for in-app purchases, earning the mobile game developer around $470 million in revenue. This is one example of how women are growing new markets and pushing for better customer experiences.

Female gamers are on the rise, increasing the customer base for the gaming industry which includes developers and gaming equipment providers. A 2019 survey found 39 per cent of American female gamers claimed they played Pokémon Go, while a further 34 per cent had played the battle game Fortnite. In Asia, 37 per cent of total gamers are female and it is growing at a rate of 11 per cent per year, nearly double that of new male gamers.[34] Although the majority of female gamers are casual gamers, there is a growing number of female Gen Z gamers playing competitive games and esports. For example, Korean player Seo Ji-soo, or 'ToSsGirL', is one of the most successful female esports players in the world and was once considered the best female StarCraft player.[35]

The visibility and participation of women in esports is gaining more attention. All-female leagues like the Valorant Champions Tour Game Changers became the most-viewed female esports tournament in 2022, with 5.4 million hours viewed.[36] In Asia, it is attracting even more female fans and viewers, leading to larger sponsorships and endorsements. In 2019 and 2020, MAC China partnered with the popular Tencent mobile game Honor of Kings,

---

[33] 'Which Gender Plays Candy Crush More?' *Old School Gamers*. https://osgamers.com/faq/which-gender-plays-candy-crush-more

[34] 'Female gamers in Asia 2023 report'. *Niko Partners*.

[35] Alisa Barladyan. 'Seo ToSsGirL Ji-soo is the best female eSports player in StarCraft history'. *Telecom Asia Sport*. May 2022.

[36] Anna Bernardo. 'International Women's Day 2023: 5 women making waves in esports'. *Yahoo News*. March 2023.

one of the highest-grossing mobile games. The campaign included a collection of products, such as lipsticks, which sold out in a day.

Manage Finances

'I truly believe financial technology is one of, if not the most, dynamic and evolving industries in the world today–every day there's something new, revolutionary, innovative, and it is the sector which has one of the highest impacts on people around the globe.'[37]

—Alexandra Vidyuk, executive director, DigiDoe

To some people, Robin Hood is known as a folklore hero that stole from the rich and gave to the poor. However, to some women, Robinhood is an investing app that will make their money grow. Robinhood allows individuals to buy and sell stocks and other asset types from your smartphone without paying a commission. Robinhood reported that the number of female customers almost quadrupled between February 2020 and February 2021 and that in 2021 women made up almost 30 per cent of the app's customers.[38] The company explained that it had 'heavily invested in research on the barriers women face to investing' as it was keen to grow by encouraging more women to invest.

Women are increasingly leveraging different technological tools and platforms to take charge of their financial future, improve financial literacy, invest wisely, and make more informed financial decisions. Women have proven to be strong savers, prudent borrowers, and loyal customers, making fintech products a match made in heaven as they make it easier to save and borrow

---

[37] Interview with Alexandra Vidyuk. *eWeek UK*. April 2022.

[38] Caitlin Mullen. 'Pandemic has more women putting money into the stock market'. *The Business Women*. April 2021.

with a variety of different financial providers. The 2021 World Bank Global Financial Inclusion Index shows that the pandemic expanded access to and use of digital financial services among women. Around 77 per cent of the Asia-Pacific Economic Cooperation (APEC) region's female population, aged fifteen years old and above, made or received a digital payment in 2021.[39] This represented a surge of 14 per cent from 2017. With more women having access to mobile phones, fintech companies have responded with mobile financial services such as Safaricom's M-Pesa and M-Kesho in Kenya, and Ant-financial services in China. Apps like Mint, YNAB (You Need a Budget), and Personal Capital enable women to plan and save by setting budgets and tracking expenses. Several apps focus on financial health, offering advice on improving credit scores, reducing debt, and achieving financial wellness.

Women in business are particularly benefitting from the tidal wave of digital payment services. In developing or rural economies, women may use specialized apps or platforms that offer microloans, savings accounts, and financial services tailored to small-scale entrepreneurs and individuals with limited access to traditional banking. Cantilan Bank (CANBNK), a rural bank in the Philippines, serves twelve provinces in Visayas and Eastern Mindanao, where poverty levels are high. Through digitalization, the bank increased their female client base by more than 60 per cent.[40] In 2019, CANBNK became the country's first bank to go live on a cloud-based banking system with support from the country's central bank. They began using tablets out in remote

---

[39] Rhea Crisologo Hernando. 'Narrowing the Gender Gap in Access to Digital Finance Can Help Women to Thrive'. *Asia-Pacific Economic Co-operation*. March 2023.

[40] 'Is Digital Finance the Answer to Giving Women-Owned MSMEs Access to Credit?' *Development Asia*. January 2023. https://development.asia/insight/ digital-finance-answer-giving-women-owned-msmes-access-credit

areas and two years later launched a mobile app delivering cashless financial services to underbanked communities.

Manage Health

> 'This is an exciting time for the role of technology in medical practice–we've seen it play an important and helpful part of patient care during the pandemic.'[41]
>
> —Laura Yecies, CEO, Bone Health Technologies

Digitalization is making healthcare services for women of all ages more accessible and of better quality, in both developed and developing economies. For instance, health technologies—known as MedTech—are making it possible for women to manage their health and well-being on a more precise and personalized level than ever before. Examples range from fertility, menstruation, pregnancy, hormone, and menopause tracking apps to devices that train the pelvis. MedTech is facilitating healthcare services for women in remote, crowded, or underserved areas. For example, telemedicine platforms can connect women with doctors and specialists in real-time, reducing the need for travel and improving access to care. In the US, women aged twenty-five to forty-four are the most frequent telehealth users, while women aged forty-five to sixty-four are the most frequent users for chronic condition management.[42] Even the metaverse can benefit women who are too scared to ask for help get access to female health advice on taboo issues. We discuss more about these innovations later. The key point is that women's digital health has significant

[41] 'Interview: Bone Health Technologies CEO / Board Member Laura Yecies on MedTech, Innovation, Leadership and Travel'. *EKMH Innovators*. May 2021. https://www.ekmhinnovators.com/ekmh-innovators-blog-beta/interview-bone-health-technologies-ceo-board-laura-yecies-medtech-innovation-leadership

[42] Rebecca Pifer. 'Why are women more likely to use telehealth?' *Healthcare Dive*. November 2021.

potential and is projected to reach a global value of $6.4 billion by 2030.[43] With advances in technology, new solutions are being explored to make the detection of chronic diseases quicker and treatments more effective. For example, in 2020, there were 2.3 million women diagnosed with breast cancer and 685,000 deaths globally. Roughly half of all breast cancers occur in women with no specific risk factors other than sex and age. This makes early detection key. Wearable devices are being tested to make breast cancer detection faster, like the smart bra. iTBra detects small changes in temperature that could indicate growth of cancerous tumours. In Europe, EPFL and Icosa are testing a smart bra which uses ultrasound waves to identify tumours. When it detects a suspicious mass, it alerts the wearer via an app to get a medical check-up. In the US, a team of Massachusetts Institute of Technology (MIT) researchers have developed a wearable ultrasound scanner.[44] The home device is a flexible patch that can be attached to a bra, allowing the wearer to move an ultrasound tracker along the patch and image the breast tissue from different angles.

Manage the Home

'All of those who are offended by the household chores app are really offended by the possibility that they will have to start doing their bit at home.'[45]

—Angela Rodríguez, Secretary of State for Equality and Gender Violence of Spain

'It's your turn to empty the dishwasher!' Have you ever heard a woman say this? Even though women are more educated

---

[43] 'Women's Digital Health Market'. *Vantage Market Research*.

[44] Anne Trafton. 'MIT invented a wearable ultrasound device that detects breast cancer'. *World Economic Forum*. August 2023.

[45] Jack Guy. 'Do men shun household chores? Spain is launching an app to find out'. *CNN*. May 2023.

than a decade ago and working, they are still taking on most of the household and family duties. Even in couples with similar levels of education, time in paid work, and shared beliefs about gender roles, women still do the bulk of housework. In the UK, working-aged men spend around half as much time on domestic unpaid work as working-aged women. In Japan, men are spending just a fifth of the time spent by women on domestic tasks. However, smart technology in the home is easing the burden of those that are suffering with a lack of time by increasing convenience and safety while streamlining tasks and simplifying housework. For example, smart home devices like smart thermostats, lighting systems, and home assistants—like Amazon, Alexa, and Google Home—enable voice-activated control over household functions, making it easier to manage the home environment. Robotic vacuum cleaners can autonomously clean floors, saving time and effort. Equipped with sensors and advanced algorithms, these devices navigate your home, avoiding obstacles, and vacuum your floors. Washing machines and self-cleaning dishwashers can now be controlled remotely through smartphone apps. You can start or schedule cleaning cycles from anywhere, making household chores more convenient than ever.

The move to a 'smart home' could shift the household burden away from women and encourage more men to take on house duties. Historically, the rise of domestic appliances in the 1950s has been associated with women playing a bigger role in the labour market. Today, with IoT, developing smart technologies are increasingly being introduced by men. American industry sales figures from 2021 show that consumers of smart home devices are more likely to be male.[46] However, millennial women aged between eighteen to thirty-five are particularly excited about smart home technology and in some instances more interested in some

---

[46] Yolande Strengers and Jenny Kennedy. 'Why smart home devices and feminized A.I. need a rethink'. *Slate*. September 2020.

devices than men are, such as voice assistants and some smart appliances. In China, JD.com found that Chinese female shoppers are more likely to acquire high-tech household appliances—such as floor-cleaning robots and dishwashers—and have a stronger preference for energy-saving products, making them an important target audience for home gadget brands.[47]

In the US, associate professors Elizabeth J. Altman and Beth Humberd explored how AI could help with the day-to-day tasks and responsibilities of running a household—and whether this powerful technology could reduce the gender inequality around housework.[48] Their view is that AI might not help with gender equality of time spent on household chores, but it could reduce the mental burden for women. 'AI is likely to provide some time-saving, but we think that the unique promise is in reducing some of the cognitive and mental load. Personally, I'm always multitasking, thinking of the "other thing." If I have a break in between classes, I'm at work thinking, "Oh, let me schedule that doctor's appointment for my kids' annual physicals."'[49]

To ease the mental load, there are many apps and software designed for household management, task scheduling, and chore tracking. In Spain, the government has gone a step further and has launched a new free app which allows each member of the household to track how much time they spend on domestic chores.[50] Angela Rodríguez, second-in-command in Spain's Ministry of Equality, explained that 'it's a very simple thing' as the app called *Me Toca* (My Turn) will work in a similar way to apps

[47] Xiaoqian Han and Doris Liu. 'JD.com Data: Women's Consumption Increasingly Focuses on Own Needs'. *JD Retail*. March 2022.

[48] Elizabeth J. Altman and Beth Humberd. 'The gendered division of household labour and emerging technologies'. *The Brookings Institution*. September 2023.

[49] Ed Brennen. 'Women Still Do More Housework Than Men. Can AI Help?' *University of Melbourne*. September 2023.

[50] Jack Guy. 'Do men shun household chores? Spain is launching an app to find out'. *CNN*. May 2023.

like Splitwise, which allow groups to share the cost of meals or other spending.

Save the Planet

> 'Women make more sustainable lifestyle choices, and are 10% more inclined than men to learn about sustainability.'[51]
>
> —GetSmarter Report

Women generally tend to care more about the planet than men. This finding is consistent in psychological research.[52] Market research firm Mintel has termed an 'eco gender gap', where green branding tends to cater to women that are more environmentally conscious. Rachel Howell from the University of Edinburgh finds that 'Women have higher levels of socialisation to care about others and be socially responsible, which then leads them to care about environmental problems and be willing to adopt environmental behaviours.'[53] Further, women have a higher demand for sustainability-focused roles,[54] with 58 per cent of sustainability executives in large companies being female.[55]

Based on the need to save the planet, women are developing climate tech solutions to manage greenhouse gas emissions. The year 2023 was described as the hottest year ever recorded and scientists say that temperatures will keep rising. The extreme weather conditions

---

[51] 'Living a Sustainable Lifestyle: How Women are Leading the Movement'. *GetSmarter*. September 2021.

[52] Jessica E. Desrochers, Graham Albert, Taciano Milfont, Benjamin Kelly, Steven Arnocky. 'Does personality mediate the relationship between sex and environmentalism?' *Personality and Individual Differences*. Vol. 147.

[53] E. Hunt. 'The eco gender gap: why is saving the planet seen as women's work?' *The Guardian*. February 2020.

[54] 'Sustainability: The Meaning, Changing Perceptions, and Expanding Agendas'. *GetSmarter*. September 2021.

[55] J. Klein. 'Women in sustainability on starting their careers and making change'. *GreenBiz*. August 2020.

throughout the year created a lot of damage and loss of lives. The 2023 Hawaii wildfires killed over 110 people in the town of Lahaina. A record-breaking heat wave in Asia affected multiple countries, including India, China, Laos, and Thailand. Storm Daniel affected Greece, Bulgaria, and Turkey with extensive flooding. To mitigate the adverse effects of climate change and adapt, entrepreneurial women have taken it upon themselves to innovate and develop digital solutions ranging from renewable energy to tech solutions to manage waste, reduce carbon emissions, and improve food security. For instance, Molly Morse, founder of Mango Materials, has developed a technology that transforms methane into biodegradable plastic pellets that can be implemented in any supply chain and eventually decompose on their own.[56] Jennifer Wagner, from CarbonCure, is working with concrete.[57] Cement production is responsible for about 8 per cent of the world's carbon footprint. CarbonCure is working to reduce its carbon footprint by injecting recycled carbon dioxide into concrete and making it stronger and more affordable in the process.

The puzzling question is: why are men, in general as consumers, less involved in saving the planet? New Zealand researchers think that the lack of conscientiousness in men may be partly responsible. Hence, companies and government agencies should focus on initiatives aimed at increasing men's awareness towards protecting the environment. The eco-gender gap can be closed by targeting products and services and activities that cater to men's interests. On the other hand, it is worth noting that at ministerial level and as investors of climate tech, men are overrepresented, suggesting that environmental issues are still very much high on their level of consciousness. In the 2021 UN Climate Change Conference—known as COP26—men accounted for 51 per cent of registered government delegates. They were 60 per cent of

---

[56] Irene Boghdadi. 'Biofuels, Plastic and the Environment: Interview with Molly Morse, CEO, Mango Materials.' *CleanTech Group*. April 2020.

[57] CarbonCure website https://www.carboncure.com/news/carboncures-jennifer-wagner-named-a-climate-trailblazer/

the active speakers in the plenary and spoke for 74 per cent of the time.[58] The OECD took a look at environmental ministries around the world and found the gender gap in decision making to be widest in regions likely to suffer the greatest damage from climate change, and where women are most vulnerable to environmental risk.[59]

What Is the (Female) Digital Economy and Why Does it Matter?

Unlike previous industrial revolutions, the scale, scope, and speed of the fourth industrial revolution is unprecedented. Technological breakthroughs and the increasing take up of digital tools is spurring the digital economy to continue expanding. Every industry from health, education, and finance is being digitally transformed. The role of women is changing too, albeit at a slower rate. Women (just like men) are already using digital technologies to improve their daily lives but often the digital applications or devices are not adequately suited to them. The female digital revolution has only just started but there are more opportunities for equality and equity. Now that we understand what the female digital economy is, let us study the current and future digital technologies being designed and deployed, and what it means for women and young girls. In short, let us begin to understand how technologies can deliver greater opportunities.

---

[58] 'Overrepresentation of Men in UN Climate Process Persists'. *United Nations Climate Change*. September 2021.

[59] Sigita Strumskyte, Sara Ramos Magaña, Helene Bendig. 'Women's leadership in environmental action'. *OECD Environment Working Papers*. No. 193. April 2022.

Chapter 2

Technology for Women

'If every woman in the world had a smartphone, it would transform their lives.'[1]

—Melinda Gates, philanthropist

Liz Salcedo's smartphone constantly ran out of charge. Working as a social worker, she got frustrated when her phone wouldn't last until the afternoon. She became so fed up that she decided to take matters into her own hands. Using off-the-shelf components, Salcedo and her husband managed to build a phone charger inside her handbag. Soon after, a number of friends asked Salcedo if she could retrofit their bags. And before you knew it, she had started a company called Everpurse. For $189 you could buy a handbag that had a wire-free charging pocket inside.[2] Like Salcedo, millions of other women could not survive the day without their smartphone. Studies show that women could spend up to six hours a day on

---

[1] Melinda Gates. 'If every woman had a smartphone'. *The Economist Newspaper Ltd.* 2015.

[2] Jennifer Alsever. '4 Ways to Successfully Market Tech to Women.' *Inc.* https://www.inc.com/magazine/201404/jennifer-alsever/tech-companies-market-to-female-audience.html

their smartphones, which is more than men,[3] and that women are more addicted to their smartphones.[4] More often than not, they use their smartphones as a communication and information tool—Whatsapping colleagues, friends and family, or keeping up to date with news, or simply looking at what's new on social media.

Smartphones were first introduced in the 1990s by IBM. Frank Canova created a prototype and named it Sweetspot. It was demonstrated at a trade show and in December 1992, the first text message was sent saying 'Merry Christmas'. In 1994, it went on sale to the public.[5] Smartphones were originally meant to allow individuals to communicate via phone and email but have since evolved into handheld devices that allow people to access the internet. In 2001, mobile phones became connected to 3G networks, creating a transformational change. 3G users had access to more data, a camera on their phone, and internet service on the go. Today, smartphones are produced by large technology companies like Apple and Samsung. Over time, the cost of smartphones has fallen, making the devices accessible to people in developed and developing economies. A total of 61 per cent of women in low-middle income countries now use the internet on their mobile phones and 81 per cent own a mobile phone.[6]

Female ownership of a smartphone can be seen as the gateway to greater independence financially, socially, and in gaining employment including business opportunities. But the smartphone is not the only technology empowering women like Salcedo. There is a whole digital ecosystem that connects devices,

---

[3] 'Women more addicted to smartphones than men: Study'. *Business Today*. May 2016.

[4] 'Women are more addicted to their smartphones than men, suggests the world's biggest study on the subject. Here's what you need to know'. *Toronto Star*. December 2023.

[5] Alia Paavola. 'Smartphone history: a complete timeline'. *Textline*. December 2022.

[6] 'The Mobile Gender Gap Report 2023'. *GSMA*.

software, and equipment that is changing the female economy. In 2023, the mobile economy amounted to \$5.2 trillion of economic value added, or 5 per cent of GDP globally, and supported 28 million jobs.[7] In the following sections, we examine digital tools and solutions like digital identities, AI, blockchain, the metaverse, drones and quantum computing. We learn what the technology is, how it is being used and what impact it has for women and their economic potential.

Digital Identities

'Digital identity solutions built for everyone are built by everyone.'[8]

—Emma Lindley, co-founder, Women in Identity

The movie *Mission Impossible* introduces Ethan Hunt, an American spy who is framed for murder and tries to clear his name by finding the killer and keeping American security secrets safe. Hunt and his mentor, Jim Phelps, go on a covert American government assignment that takes a disastrous turn, leaving Jim dead and Hunt the prime murder suspect. Now a fugitive, Hunt sneaks into a heavily guarded Central Intelligence Agency Headquarters in Virginia to retrieve a confidential computer file that will prove his innocence. But the computer is located in a room that is protected with fingerprint and retina scanners, which only allow identified and verified officials into the building. The mission is impossible. To obtain the computer file, Hunt enters the computer room from above without touching anything, except the keyboard. The biometric technology used in the first 1996 movie has now

---

[7] 'The Mobile Economy 2023'. *GSMA*.

[8] Francesca Hobson. 'Cultivating diversity with Women in Identity *Co-Founder*, Emma Lindley – Podcast Episode 5'. *Ubisecure*. September 2019. https://www.ubisecure.com/podcast/emma-lindley-women-in-identity/

become a reality. Digital identities are needed, not just to enter secure buildings and offices, but also as a gateway to internet services and even smartphones.

A digital identity is like your secret code on the internet that only you know. It helps websites and computers know who you are—effectively an online representation of you. This secret code is needed whenever you log into your computer, smartphone, or access social medial platforms, like username, password, and email address. A digital identity is your key to unlock a range of online services and can be based on credentials or user information. It can even be based on your biometrics, just like in the movie *Mission Impossible*. You can now log into your smartphone by just looking at it, as facial recognition technology verifies who you are. Unfortunately, not everyone has a digital identity, and some don't even have a legal identity, making it difficult to access digital services. The United Nation's Sustainable Development Goal 16.9 states that everyone should have a legal identity by 2030. As the digital economy continues to accelerate, more people will need a digital identity if they want to access the increasing number of online services, whether it be social media or shopping apps or government portals providing social support. McKinsey predicts extending full digital ID coverage could unlock an economic value equivalent to 3–13 per cent of GDP in 2030.[9]

A common use of digital identity is for online banking. Banks now use digital identity verification technology to allow new customers to open an account by taking a picture of their state-issued ID, and then a facial recognition scan to verify the person. A digital identity allows women to access and interact with a variety of different digital services—like financial,

---

[9] Olivia White, Owen Sperling, Anu Madgavkar, James Manyika, Jacques Bughin, Deepa Mahajan and Michael McCarthy. 'Digital identification: A key to inclusive growth Report.' *McKinsey Global Institute*. April 2019.

health, education, and government services—in a secure manner. For example, in Pakistan, millions of women possess a Computerized National Identity Card (CNIC), which gives them direct access to government income support. Similarly, in India,[10] more than 99 per cent of adults are now covered by Aadhaar, the government's national biometric identity system which relies on fingerprints and iris scans to create a national identity database. Women can open bank accounts using Aadhaar's biometric information instead of relying on their husband's or brother's bank account to purchase non-household items. During the Covid-19 pandemic, any woman who opened an Aadhaar-linked Jan-Dhan savings bank account received an unconditional cash transfer of $8 per month for three months. This transfer was made to about 200 million women.[11]

Digital identities are becoming widespread and cannot be ignored. More governments are looking at how to roll out national digital identity frameworks and how they can support cross-border trade and travel. At the same time, companies are innovating with biometric technology to make our daily lives more seamless. Even paying for your groceries at the supermarket could change and become more convenient. In the US, the food store, Whole Foods, has been testing palm scanners which allows Amazon customers to pay by waving their hand. The Amazon One 'palm signature' is encrypted and securely stored in the Amazon Web Services (AWS) cloud and the palm scan cannot be replicated or used without the user's consent. With the growing

---

[10] 'India introduces economic reforms to improve women's access to markets and financial assets.' *Council for Foreign Relations*. https://www.cfr.org/womens-participation-in-global-economy/case-studies/india/

[11] Shweta Saini and Siraj Hussain. 'Leveraging India's Aadhaar platform to ease COVID-19 pain.' *East Asia Forum*. October 2021. https://www.eastasiaforum.org/2021/10/01/leveraging-indias-aadhaar-platform-to-ease-covid-19-pain/

use of different types of digital identities, going forward, your mission, should you wish to accept it, is to make digital identities inclusive and available for all.

Artificial Intelligence

'We have a chance at changing the narrative here—to create a world where people see AI as an engine for opportunity for them, to help them find access to better opportunities, to help them find better jobs, to help them find more fulfilling work.'[12]

—Nancy Xu, CEO, Moonhub

Ada Lovelace was an English mathematician in the 1800s. She was also the first computer programmer. She realized that the computer could follow a series of simple instructions—a program—to perform a complex calculation. However, the computer was never built. Instead, she wrote about what she described as 'the Analytical Engine', which, according to Lovelace, 'can do whatever we know how to order it to perform. It can follow analysis, but it has no power of anticipating any . . . relations or truths. Its province is to assist us in making available what we are already acquainted with.'[13] Lovelace was predicting the use of AI.

You can think of AI as a robot friend who can learn new things and do tasks by itself. Just like learning to ride a bike, this robot learns too, but in a different way. Instead of having to be

---

[12] Will Henshall. 'The Biggest Moments of TIME's Impact Dinner: Extraordinary Women Shaping the Future of AI.' *Time*. October 2023. https://time.com/6322589/impact-dinner-extraordinary-women-shaping-artificial-intelligence/

[13] Justyna Zwolak. 'Ada Lovelace: The World's First Computer Programmer Who Predicted Artificial Intelligence'. *National Institute of Standards and Technology*. March 2023.

told exactly what to do each time, the robot can sometimes figure things out on its own. It can look at pictures and recognize what's in them, or it can listen to what people say and understand. It's like having a really smart friend but it's all inside a computer. You may be wondering what happens inside the computer. Well, the computer processes huge volumes of data based on instructions given by you. In short, AI technology can process large amounts of data, recognize patterns, and make decisions. For example, machine learning, which is a subset of AI, uses a sequence of instructions known as algorithms—that are trained on data—to categorize images, analyse data, or predict future outcomes. In the business world, many companies are leveraging machine learning tools to enhance productivity and the customer experience. An example of this would be Amazon suggesting products to consumers based on their past purchases, or Netflix recommending what movies to watch based on your past viewing behaviour. Other examples include financial institutions using machine learning to predict stock market or price fluctuations, or schools and universities translating text from one language to another. This type of machine learning has expanded into four waves. Dr Kai-Fu Lee, an AI expert, talks about the four waves of AI.[14] The first wave is described above and is known as the 'internet wave', which collects and labels data to help learn. The second wave is the 'business wave' where AI applications are used on business data. An example of this is AI's use on bank data to understand and process business loan applications faster. The third wave is when cameras or microphones can see, hear, and sense things and make smart decisions. It includes heat sensors or movement sensors. The fourth wave is autonomous AI, with self-driving cars being a prime example.

---

[14] Dr Kai-Fu Lee, *AI Superpowers: China, Silicon Valley and The New World Order.* Houghton Mifflin Harcourt Publishing. 2018.

Given this multitude of benefits, AI-based tools can provide women with tailored information on health and safety, financial services, as well as home business solutions, and learning resources.[15] For instance, virtual assistants and chatbots can provide women with 24/7 access to medical advice, including information on sexual and reproductive health. The chatbot is an AI software tool that mimics human conversation, answering questions by processing large amounts of data to find the right answer for you. Another example is wearable devices with sensors. These sensors detect and measure physical properties and convert this information into a format that machines can understand. They serve as the eyes, ears, skin, tongue, and nose of AI systems. Examples include fitness trackers, blood pressure monitors, or fertility and menstrual trackers. Some wearables can raise the alarm on potential health risks including those related to pregnancy or breast cancer.

In terms of employment, AI job matching tools can connect women seeking job opportunities with hiring companies that align with their skills and experience. AI tools can assist in developing CVs and in preparing for job interviews, which is particularly important for women who have been out of the workforce for a long time and therefore might not have access to relevant advice. AI can even reduce gender bias in the hiring process and prevent, flag, and protect against gender-based harassment.[16] For example, AI firm NexLP has developed #MeTooBots that monitor communications between colleagues and flag bullying and sexual

[15] Neelam Mahraj. 'Empowering "Women" Through Artificial Intelligence. Artificial Intelligence in Plan English'. *Medium.* April 2023. https://ai.plainenglish.io/empowering-women-through-artificial-intelligence-9197ee2170f6

[16] Kim Thomson. 'How will AI impact women in the workplace?' *University of Melbourne.* September 2023. https://study.unimelb.edu.au/study-with-us/professional-development/blog/how-will-ai-impact-women-in-the-workplace/

harassment in documents, emails, and chat. AllVoices apps enable people to report harassment when it occurs.

AI can also support women affected by war. LifeForce is an online platform that uses algorithms to match the supply and demand of aid to mothers and single women affected by Russia's invasion of Ukraine.

> The initial product design took the needs of women and especially single mothers into account after the conscription of males into the Ukrainian resistance effort, as did the design of its analytics, the prioritization of product creation.[17]

In other words, the app facilitates a coordinated response providing immediate support, advice, and real time content on a secure platform to those who are most affected in Ukraine.

Just like Lovelace, women continue to innovate using AI. Mira Murati is the modern-day Ada. Murati developed ChatGPT, an AI chatbot that uses natural language processing to create humanlike conversational dialogue. As the chief technology officer (CTO), at the American company OpenAI, Murati led a team that developed the tool.[18] Murati co-founded the company OpenAI with Sam Altman, Ilya Sutskever, and Greg Brockman, which is expected to be the third most valuable tech company in the world.

Murati was born in Albania and studied Mechanical Engineering at Dartmouth College, the US university where the AI discipline was born. Before joining OpenAI, she was an analyst at Goldman Sachs, an engineer at French aerospace company Zodiac Aerospace, a product manager at Tesla—where she oversaw the Model X—and vice president of product at

---

[17] Chloe Laws. 'Can artificial intelligence really advance gender equality?' *Glamour.* May 2023.

[18] 'Mira Murati – the woman behind AI tool ChatGPT.' *Women in Tech.*

Leap Motion—a virtual reality company. Murati has become a celebrity and was interviewed by Trevor Noah on *The Daily Show*. On the show, Murati said, 'The magic is just understanding the patterns and analysing the patterns between a lot of information, a lot of training data that we have fed into this system.' She was talking about DALL·E, the first version of an AI system that she helped to develop, which creates realistic images and art from a description in natural language. More than 3 million people are already using DALL·E to extend their creativity and speed up their workflows, generating over 4 million images a day.[19]

Murat's influence and groundbreaking work on AI has been recognized in *Financial Times'* list of the '25 Most Influential Women of 2023'. In her interview with Noah, she emphasized that the conversation around AI must be inclusive:

> The technology shapes us and we shape it (. . .) There are a lot of ethical and philosophical questions that we need to consider. And it's important that we bring in different voices, like philosophers, social scientists, artists, and people from the humanities.[20]

AI will continue to fundamentally change the way people collect and process data, transforming business and public operations across different industries and public services. Some have described the revolution as the invention of electricity.[21] Having more women like Murati lead AI design and development will bring greater diversity to prevent biases and enhance the technology's ethical standards. We discuss the importance of

---

[19] 'DALL·E API now available in public beta'. *OpenAI*. November 2022.

[20] 'Mira Murati - DALL·E 2 and the Power of AI'. *The Daily Show*. https://www.youtube.com/watch?v=Ba_C-C6UwlI

[21] Dr Kai-Fu Lee. *AI Superpowers: China, Silicon Valley and The New World Order*. Houghton Mifflin Harcourt Publishing. 2018.

this in greater detail in the next chapter where we unearth the problems with biased algorithms and the importance of female representation.

The Metaverse

'Our initiative in the metaverse allows women with issues related to their intimate health to come and learn and exchange on the subject.'[22]

—Tracy Cohen Sayag, president,
Clinique des Champs-Élysées

On 28 October 2021, Mark Zuckerberg, the CEO of Facebook, introduced Meta.[23] Zuckerberg said that Meta's focus will be to bring the metaverse to life and help people connect, find communities, and grow businesses. Since the announcement a number of different metaverse platforms have facilitated fashion shows, music concerts, meetings and even weddings. The metaverse has the scope to be so much more than just entertainment—from creating jobs to providing virtual learning opportunities. This is music to the ears of women who enjoy or only have access to remote working and learning.

The metaverse can be described as a digital playground, where people can play, learn, work, and hang out together, all without leaving their homes. Wearing a head-mounted device, you can visit different places, cities, or museums, meet new friends, and even create your own career in the metaverse. For example, jobs in the metaverse include virtual tour guides, community managers, software engineers, 3D modellers and

[22] David Marsanic. 'Women's Health in the Metaverse: French Clinic Hosts Landmark Event'. *Daily Coin.* April 2023. https://dailycoin.com/women-health-in-metaverse-french-clinic-hosts-landmark-event/

[23] 'Introducing Meta: A Social Technology Company'. *Meta.* October 2021.

event directors. The metaverse is a three-dimensional virtual space that uses a computer-generated environment with scenes and objects, described as virtual reality (VR). It can even be just like the real world as augmented reality technology (AR) allows for enhanced interaction through real-time text, graphics, and sound.

In the metaverse, female students can enter the educational environment without being constrained by time or place, enabling them to engage with various objects in real time. Women can feel as if they are in a real classroom, and there is a growing demand for this experience. The size of the global market for VR and AR in the education sector is expected to reach $29 billion by 2030, with a Compound Annual Growth Rate (CAGR) of 40 per cent during the forecast period of 2022 to 2030.[24] This growth includes professional education in a virtual environment. For instance, the platform Osso VR provides realistic, hands-on surgical training simulations that allow medical students to practice procedures in a risk-free environment, improving skill development and patient outcomes. This learning approach can improve access to millions of young girls and women, who are unable to leave their homes, as well as females in remote and rural areas. Given these social benefits, entrepreneurial women are taking advantage of the metaverse. For instance, Sophia Technologies offers students in over twenty-four countries an online British education programme. It is now venturing into the metaverse.[25] The company founded in 2018 by CEO Melissa McBride, partnered with Athena Labs Immersive Virtual Reality

---

[24] 'Augmented Reality & Virtual Reality Market for Education Industry - Industry Analysis, Market Size, Share, Trends, Application Analysis, Growth And Forecast 2024-2030.' IndustryARC.

[25] 'The Female Founded Start-up that is Shaping Education in the Metaverse'. *Yahoo News*. March 2022.

and now plans to reshape the 'education experience' for children all over the world.

The metaverse is more likely to benefit women in the first instance. Compared to men, women are interacting in the metaverse to a greater extent. McKinsey found that in 2022, 41 per cent of women used a primary metaverse platform or participated in a digital world for more than a year, compared to only 34 per cent of men.[26] Thirty-five per cent of the women surveyed were power users, which means they spend more than three hours a week in the metaverse, compared to 29 per cent of men.

With more women than men using a metaverse platform, there is scope for women to improve their health, express themselves, and travel in safe and intimate settings.[27] As mentioned before, women's digital health provides access to health information and the metaverse can be seen as an extension of that service. For example, with an experienced team of health specialists, a clinic in France hosted its first ever event in the metaverse to break the taboo surrounding women's health issues. With one click to attend, the women participating were able to interact with doctors through chat, video, and voice, discussing topics like pregnancy, menopause, and the impact of chemotherapy treatments. Metaverse hospitals could also improve women's access to healthcare. In the UAE, the development of the Thumbay healthcare facility is aiming to create a virtual hospital where people will come with an avatar and consult with the doctor.[28]

---

[26] Mina Alaghband and Lareina Yee. 'Even in the metaverse, women remain locked out of leadership roles'. *McKinsey & Company*. November 2022.

[27] Paola Peralta. 'There is an enormous gender imbalance in the metaverse industry'. *Benefit News*. April 2023.

[28] Paulina Okunytė. 'UAE to Launch World's First Hospital in the Metaverse'. *Daily Coin*. July 2022. https://dailycoin.com/uae-to-launch-worlds-first-hospital-in-the-metaverse/

Patients can see what the hospital looks like in the metaverse before travelling in-person to the facility. Furthermore, the metaverse could improve the quality of women's mental health. A health platform company called XRHealth trialled mental health treatments using VR in a patient's own home. The research involved sixty-one participants who exclusively received 'virtual retail therapy', solely in the metaverse. The VR study provided the participants with relaxing environments, encouraged controlled breathing, promoted mindfulness, and improved physical fitness. Post-treatment, participants noted a 34 per cent reduction in anxiety and noted a 32 per cent decrease in stress levels.[29]

The metaverse offers an opportunity for women to participate in an equal and inclusive environment. Unlike many real-world industries where gender biases persist, the metaverse allows individuals to express themselves and engage with others based on their ideas, skills, and creativity. Through the power of digital avatars, women can be free from stereotypes. The metaverse facilitates connections between women from different backgrounds and cultures who share similar goals and interests.[30] Metaverse projects such as World of Women, Women in Web3, and Women in Tech are collaborative, decentralized ecosystems where women can create, exhibit, and monetize their unique digital artworks.

An inclusive metaverse environment can encourage women to learn new sports. Women are much more hesitant to try a new sport compared to men, due to the fear of embarrassment. The metaverse can change this and make it easier for women to stay active and engaged, as they can participate in their favourite activities without having to leave their homes. Some women

---

[29] 'XRHealth's Virtual Reality Therapy Shows Promise for Mental Health Therapy in the Metaverse'. *NFTevening*. October 2023. https://nftevening.com/xrhealths-virtual-reality-therapy-shows-promise-for-mental-health-therapy-in-the-metaverse/

[30] 'Empowering women: unlocking new opportunities in Web3 and the metaverse'. *The Sandbox*. June 2017.

are already turning to VR headsets to get fit. Influencer Clarke Peoples, who's known for lifestyle and beauty content, shared her own VR workout with her 500,000 followers, who described the workout as the 'peloton of the metaverse'.[31]

Blockchain Technology

'In blockchain, we are building equality in the technology. In blockchain, crypto, web 3.0, we're building a new economy, a new ecosystem.'[32]

—Lisa Wade, CEO, Digital X

Coffee is one of Rwanda's most significant exports. The majority of it is exported to Germany as it boasts of aromatic flavours.[33] German missionaries first introduced the crop into German East Africa in 1905. Since then, it has a history of economic dependence on the agricultural development of coffee. Many female farmers work on Rwanda's coffee plantations but are often underpaid. To increase their wages, the International Women's Coffee Alliance (IWCA) partnered with blockchain programmes and initiatives to create a technological solution. Using blockchain technology, IWCA made the supply chain for Rwandan coffee scalable and transparent.

Blockchain technology is like a notebook where you write down all the transactions you make. Each time you make a

---

[31] Jordan Hart. 'Move over teenage gamers – women wanting to get fit are the new frontier for VR headsets'. *The Business Insider.* July 2023. https://www. businessinsider.com/more-women-using-vr-headsets-for-workouts-company-says-2023-7

[32] Simran Jagdev. 'Women in Blockchain: Where We Are, and The Way Forward'. *Consensys.* March 2022.

[33] Shailey Singh. 'How blockchain empowers women in developing economies'. *Coin Telegraph.* March 2023. https://cointelegraph.com/explained/how-blockchain-empowers-women-in-developing-economies

transaction, you write it down along with the time the transaction took place and who you traded with. Now, imagine, instead of just having one notebook there are thousands of copies of this notebook spread out all over the world, and everyone has a copy. Therefore, if you want to add a new transaction to your notebook, you need to tell everyone. They check their own copies of the notebook to make sure your transaction is legitimate. If they all agree, they add your transaction to their notebooks too. That's kind of how a blockchain works.

Blockchain technology or distributed ledger keeps confidential information like personal records, contracts, and payments safe. It provides a transparent and unchangeable list of transactions. For instance, the coffee produced by Rwandan female farmers can now be tracked to its origin. The traceable digital record enables female workers to obtain a higher market price in the export market and ensure that female farmers get their fair share of the sales revenue. The initiative has been successful with multinational companies like Nestlé taking a similar approach. In 2020, Nestlé started exploring blockchain supply chain and launched a limited edition blockchain coffee beans pilot project from three countries—Brazil, Rwanda, and Colombia.

Blockchain technology can also create secure digital identities, which is especially important for women who don't have official identification documents. With blockchain, disadvantaged women can access support services and prove their identity. For example, the World Food Programme uses a blockchain-based platform—Building Blocks—to provide women who are running households in Bangladesh with support to buy nutritious food and menstrual hygiene and reproductive health products.[34] Building Blocks is a collection of

---

[34] Vincent Matak. 'How blockchain can power efforts to empower women and girls in Bangladesh'. *World Food Programme*. December 2022. https://www.wfp.org/stories/how-blockchain-can-power-efforts-to-empower-women-and-girls-bangladesh

computer servers independently operated by each participating organization but connected together to allow humanitarian organizations to coordinate assistance. In Bangladesh, the platform allows women to collect food and personal items at the same time from local retail outlets using a QR code, rather than collecting from different organizations at separate locations with different methods of verification.

Blockchain also has the potential to assist women in buying land and property. The technology provides a secure and undisputable record of property ownership, making it more difficult for property rights to be denied. In some parts of the world, women face challenges in asserting and protecting property rights. Blockchain can overcome this challenge. One woman who is simplifying the home purchasing process is Natalia Karayaneva.[35] Her company, Propy, in Silicon Valley introduced smart contracts and automation to help brokers and estate agents migrate to a paperless deal-closing process, reducing the scope for fraud and ensuring transparency in property rights and title transfers. Propy plans to expand into developing economies, enabling more women to access opportunities to invest in land ownership for greater independence.

Drones

'The focus of the female gender provides countless new uses and solutions for drone technology and expands business opportunities in the current market.'[36]

—Leyre Escalante, founder, Drone e-Learning LLC

---

[35] Shailey Singh. 'How blockchain empowers women in developing economies.' *Coin Telegraph*. March 2023.

[36] 'Leyre Escalante is the founder of Drone e-Learning LLC'. *Women and Drones*. https://womenanddrones.com/leyre-escalante-venezuelan-stem-is-the-founder-of-drone-e-learning-llc/

Is it a bird? Is it a plane? No, it's a drone! A drone is a flying robot that can be remotely controlled. While drones have been used for recreational purposes, the high-resolution cameras and sensors fitted in them allows them to capture intricate details, especially in remote areas where people can't enter or reach. Drones were first used for military missions that were 'dull, dirty, or dangerous'. However, the technology can be used across different industries, including agriculture, construction, environmental monitoring, search and rescue, surveillance, and delivery services. As a result, drones are creating job opportunities for women. Many are training to become drone pilots, where they are responsible for maintaining drones, planning flight paths, assembling maps, and gathering data, footage, and digital images. For instance, Ruth Mtuwa is a drone pilot from Malawi. She is an engineer who co-founded the company DroneX Technologies.[37] Mtuwa's company uses drone technology to develop sustainable solutions within her local community. It uses drones to oversee farms to manage crop health and also, to oversee waste management in landfills.

Due to the variety of applications, the number of women in the US training to become drone licenced pilots has increased from 793 in 2016 to 24,293 in 2022.[38] In India, the government announced a training scheme to provide drones to women self-help groups as part of a larger objective to support women in agriculture.[39] In 2023, the Prime Minister of India announced that

[37] 'African women in STEM: using drone technology to boost development in Africa'. *United Nations*. https://www.un.org/osaa/news/african-women-stem-using-drone-technology-boost-development-africa

[38] 'Demographics'. *Women and Drones*.

[39] 'Indian PM says women self-help groups will be given drones; new scheme soon'. *The Hindu Business Line*. August 2023. https://www.thehindubusinessline.com/economy/agri-business/indian-pm-says-women-self-help-groups-will-be-given-drones-new-scheme-soon/article67197928.ece

15,000 women would be given loans and training for operating and repairing drones. The six-day training course aims to give village women the opportunity to earn at least $1,500 per year.[40] Globally, community platforms like Women and Drones[41] and Women Who Drone[42] are training women and assisting them to find career opportunities using drones.

The innovative use of drones in commercial businesses is giving women the chance to lead in new sectors. For example, online customers in some cities in the US have the option to get their packages delivered by a drone. Lauren Kisser is the director of Amazon Prime Air, a delivery system from Amazon that sends packages to customers in thirty minutes or less using drones. Kisser explains:

> I get to work with an amazing team that is building the future. Day-to-day, I lead the team by overseeing a mixture of business operations, programme management, engineering operations and flight testing. It's busy but really rewarding.[43]

With plans to expand Prime Air to the UK and Italy, Kisser's days will continue to stay busy.

Finally, drones can even become the eyes and ears of a police officer, giving women walking alone at night or in unfamiliar areas an extra layer of security. Drones equipped with cameras can record video footage that may be useful in case of an incident. In the UK, a system was trialled at Nottingham University to

---

[40] Rahul Karmakar. 'Drones fuel the dreams of rural women in Assam'. *The Hindu*. October 2023. https://www.thehindu.com/news/national/drones-fuel-the-dreams-of-rural-women-in-assam/article67393200.ece

[41] Women and Drones website: https://womenanddrones.com/

[42] Women Who Drone website: https://www.womenwhodrone.co/

[43] Adam Care. 'From Disney to Amazon's drone programme - Lauren Kisser on tech firm's "eye to the future"'. *Cambridge News*. December 2016.

protect students and staff on campus.[44] Controlled from an app, the drones are fitted with AI technology, thermal cameras, and a spotlight. Each drone would flood light onto the scene and stream video footage to deter or apprehend an attacker. In Mumbai, to protect women from violent attacks, the police have already deployed drones to keep an eye on the general public in risky areas after hours.[45]

Quantum Computing

'Throughout my career, I found people often underestimate female scientists.'[46]
—Professor Michelle Simmons, director of the Centre of Excellence for Quantum Computation and Communication Technology

Technology moves at a fast pace. There are already future technologies being developed and tested. One example is quantum computers. They are still in the early stages of development, but despite the technical challenges, these computers have the potential to transform sectors such as finance, logistics, as well as accelerate AI, improve cybersecurity, and manage climate change.[47] Countries like China, Japan, and South Korea are actively investing in research and development, including building quantum infrastructure.

---

[44] Michael Gibbard. 'Plan to introduce drones to help women feel safer at night'. *Walk Easy Alarms*. November 2022. https://wealarms.co.uk/drones-could-help-women-feel-safer-at-night/

[45] Kritika Kukreja. 'Mumbai Police to Get Drones For Improved Safety Of Women'. *Curly Tales*. November 2018. https://curlytales.com/mumbai-police-to-get-drones-for-improved-safety-of-women/

[46] 'Quantum leap for women'. *The Australian*.

[47] 'Encourage more women in quantum computing to foster diversity and inclusion, says Dr Ines de Vega'. *IQM*. July 2023.

You may be wondering what is so special about these computers. You can think of it like a digital library with instant access to a massive number of books. In a regular library, you look through each book one by one until you find the one you need. Now, consider a library where you can open all the books at once and find the information you need instantly. That's what quantum computers can do. They don't have to go through problems step-by-step like regular computers. Instead, they use quantum bits, or 'qubits', which can represent many possibilities at once. These qubits can be in multiple states simultaneously, which allows quantum computers to explore many solutions at the same time.

In the race to develop the advanced computer is Professor Michelle Simmons. The woman who was crowned Australian of the Year in 2018, and who received the 2023 Prime Minister's Prize for Science, set up the company Silicon Quantum Computing which is on a mission to 'build the world's first error corrective quantum computer' in Australia.[48] Simmons has pioneered unique technologies internationally to build electronic devices.[49] Simmons explains that 'every industry that relies on data will be impacted by quantum computing,' whether it's the airline industry looking to reduce fuel costs, or the agriculture industry trying to make more efficient fertilizers.

Quantum computers can solve certain types of problems exponentially faster, like drug development. New drugs cost an average of $2 billion and take more than ten years to reach the market. Quantum computing could make drug discovery, drug design, and toxicity testing more efficient by reducing the reliance on trial and error and finding and combining entire new molecules

---

[48] 'Professor Michelle Simmons: 2023 Prime Minister's Prize for Science'. *Department of Industry, Science and Resources*. https://www.youtube.com/watch?v=6VKJPCAWxX0

[49] James Dargan. '12 Women Pioneering the World of Quantum Computing'. *The Quantum Insider*. February 2020.

by analysing vast amounts of data.[50] The different applications and the improved efficiency of quantum computing has the potential to benefit women, from more effective drugs for women-related illnesses to supporting women working on farms affected by climate change. For example, quantum computing could reduce the impact of extreme weather conditions and reduce carbon emissions. Its method of simultaneous (rather than sequential) calculation could be successful in analysing weather patterns, which consist of a complex system of variables.[51] Such advances can benefit women, particularly in developing economies, who are more exposed to the impacts of climate change. In many societies, women are responsible for household energy, food, water, and family care—all of which can be destroyed in extreme flooding, heatwaves, or cyclones.[52]

To shape these benefits, talented women from STEM like Simmons are leading the way to ensure that this developing technology promotes diversity and inclusivity. Rebecca Krauthamer is another such woman—the founder of the startup called Quantum, which develops technologies for all things quantum: quantum AI, quantum molecular simulation, and quantum financial modelling.[53] The company is currently working with clients on chemical simulation, medical imaging, cryptography, and on blockchain technologies. It's also developed an educational

---

[50] Dr Mark van Rijmenam, CSP. 'How quantum computing will change the world'. *The Digital Speaker.* June 2022. https://www.thedigitalspeaker.com/quantum-computing-change-world/

[51] Stephen Gossett and Brennan Whitfield. '10 Quantum Computing Applications and Examples'. *Builtin.* June 2022.

[52] 'Five Reasons Why Climate Action Needs Women'. *UN Climate Change.* March 2023.

[53] Olivia Lam. 'Female Excellence in Quantum Computing'. *Witi.* April 2023. https://witi.com/articles/2071/Female-Excellence-in-Quantum-Computing/

programme to train people to code on quantum computers.[54] Krauthamer says that the idea of the company 'was to help build a bridge to commercial viability for the many brilliant ideas coming out of academia'.

But more women are needed in this field, especially if the global industry is expected to grow from $13.67 billion in 2022 to $143.44 billion by 2032, at a CAGR of 26 per cent.[55] According to a report by the London School of Economics and Political Science, fewer than 2 per cent of applicants for quantum jobs are female. Dr Ines de Vega, Head of Quantum Innovation at IQM Quantum Computers, says: 'I believe that because quantum is relatively new field with a great expansion potential, we have amazing chances to, this time, do it better and promote and encourage more women to follow the quantum career.'[56]

In this regard, Nithyasri Srivathsan established SheQuantum—a global quantum computing e-learning platform educating women and girls in quantum technologies.[57] The online community consists of sixty-five countries, 289 institutions and research labs, with 54 per cent of its users being women. Srivathsan, who has given numerous public speeches, and is based in Singapore, says:

---

[54] 'Rebecca Krauthamer'. *Forbes Profile.* https://www.forbes.com/profile/rebecca-krauthamer/?sh=11a6078d771c

[55] 'Quantum Computing Market'. *Spherical Insights.* https://www.sphericalinsights.com/reports/quantum-computing-market

[56] Michael Sarpong Bruce. 'IQM's Head of Innovation: Encourage More Women in Quantum Computing To Foster Diversity And Inclusion'. *The Quantum Insider.* July 2023. https://thequantuminsider.com/2023/07/19/iqms-head-of-innovation-encourage-more-women-in-quantum-computing-to-foster-diversity-and-inclusion/

[57] SheQuantum website: https://shequantum.org/

Two things meaningfully matter to me in diverse ways—quantum computing and women and when I started my quantum journey, I realized that there are puzzlingly many resources to learn from but to be very honest, I remember how much effort it takes to find the right resource for you . . . As a young woman myself, I recognized that this field is lacking talented professionals, more so women! This inspired me to make the quantum journey of other women (and men) accessible and much less of a struggle.[58]

As a result, Srivathsan authored *Quantum Computing: An [Unconventional Beginners'] Book* in 2020, which was honoured by BookAuthority twice as 'Best Quantum Computing Books for Beginners' and 'All Time Best Quantum Computing Books', recognized internationally.

> What are the technologies that are transforming women's lives?

> To sum up, there are a number of different types of digital technologies that are already being used by women, from devices, wearables and apps, to drones, blockchain and AI. There are some technologies—like quantum computing—that are still being developed and have the potential to revolutionize our lives and our industries even further. This digital revolution has the potential to drive further changes in the role of women, closing the gender gap, and bring greater equity. By zooming in on these technologies, we can ensure that we seize the opportunities that can benefit billions of women. If we don't, then there is a real risk of missed opportunities.

---

[58] SheQuantum website https://shequantum.org/nithyasri-srivathsan-4/

Chapter 3

The 'Missed' Opportunity

'There would be more GDP . . . [and] higher living standards in the world if there were more women participating in the labour force.'[1]

—Caroline Atkinson, head of global policy, Google Inc.

Evelyn Quan, a laundry owner, finds herself in a new world in *Everything Everywhere All at Once*. One minute she is living a regular life and the next she is transported to multiple universes. She and her husband, Waymond, are being audited by the tax authorities and at a tense meeting with them, Evelyn's husband is taken over by Alpha-Waymond, a version of Waymond from the 'Alphaverse'. Alpha-Waymond explains to Evelyn that many parallel universes exist because every life choice creates a new alternative universe. The sci-fi movie touches on missed opportunities. In other words, for every action you take, a different version of you might be experiencing the option that you did not choose. Middle-aged, Evelyn looks back at paths untravelled, while heading into chaos and uncertainty. To survive, she must use her new powers, 'verse-jumping technology', which allows her

---

[1] 'Interview with Caroline Atkinson'. *Council of Foreign Relations*. https://www.cfr.org/womens-participation-in-global-economy/interviews/caroline-atkinson/

to access skills, memories, and bodies of her paralleled lives and connect with different versions of herself. The movie ends on a note of hope and possibility with improved family relationships.[2] The female digital revolution is a missed opportunity, and its potential can be seen in its own Alphaverse. Similar to Evelyn, there is hope and possibility for all women and girls to have many different options to choose from, and to benefit from a higher standard of living.

Foregone opportunities are the choices we didn't make. In economics, the concept is known as 'opportunity cost', that is, the future benefits or cost that would have been gained or incurred if the alternative was chosen. In the female digital economy, the opportunity cost of not having women represented is significant. Women make up half of the global population. As digital technologies evolve, there is a real risk that women, from all walks of life, are left behind. There is a danger that they are missing out on future careers and higher incomes. There is also concern that the strong purchasing power of women is being forgotten. Women as consumers make over 80 per cent of household decisions on a daily basis.[3] In 2020, American women accounted for 73 per cent of the country's consumer spending.[4] By 2028, women across the globe are projected to own 75 per cent of discretionary spending.[5] Yet, their consumer needs are being unmet. Many female consumers spend hours scrolling online looking for the right products or services, or reading reviews on where to buy specific products.

---

[2] Jeff Yang. 'For us weird Asians, "Everything Everywhere All at Once" is a second chance'. *Washington Post*. March 2023.

[3] Krystle M. Davis. '20 Facts And Figures To Know When Marketing To Women.' *Forbes*. December 2021.

[4] Jasmin Diaz. 'The Role of Women in Driving Tech Trends.' *Women in Tech Resources and Blog*. February 2024.

[5] Sandy Carter. 'Who Runs The World? Women Control 85% Of Purchases, 29% Of STEM Roles.' *Forbes*. March 2024.

For businesses, this is a missed opportunity to innovate and create tailored products for women and to increase their customer base.[6]

The cost of the untapped potential of including women in the digital economy was estimated to be $94 billion in the APEC region in 2020[7]. This is a missed economic opportunity, especially since around 900 million women in the world don't have access to mobile internet. Almost two-thirds of these women live in South Asia and Sub-Saharan Africa or live in remote or rural areas.[8] The unequal access to mobile technology has been termed as the 'digital divide'. As mentioned in the first chapter, World Economic Forum Founder, Klaus, introduced the concept of the fourth industrial revolution, but he did so with concern and recognized that the technological progress would increase inequality. Closing the gender gap in using mobile internet in low-middle income economies could deliver an additional $700 billion in GDP growth by 2028. Next, we highlight the different missed opportunities. We discuss how women could potentially miss out on good jobs with higher pay, innovation that caters to their needs, better investor returns on women-led businesses, and better policies and regulation to reduce online harm.

More Jobs, Better Pay

'Tech's influence is only going to deepen, which makes ensuring a diverse workforce even more paramount—both for giving women and other underrepresented groups access to high-paying jobs, and for ensuring that technology functions

---

[6] Aiste Araminaite-Pivore. 'Why We Need More Gender Diversity in the Tech Industry'. *AV Network*. November 2023. https://www.avnetwork.com/blogs/why-we-need-more-gender-diversity-in-the-tech-industry

[7] 'The Untapped Economic Potential of Including Women in the Digital Economy in the APEC Region'. *APEC Policy Partnership on Women and the Economy*. September 2022.

[8] 'The Mobile Gender Gap Report 2023'. *GSMA*.

equitably. A diverse tech sector will help build more diverse societies as well.'[9]

—Professor Susan Athey,
Stanford Graduate School of Business

Swapna Bakshi is a mobile app tester. She tests the backend side of a finance app. She makes sure that everything displayed on the app is correct and there are no interruptions when sending data. In an interview, she spoke about why she chose this role:

> If I am being totally honest with you, I didn't want to go into technology, I wanted to study Social Science, but my father wanted me to pursue a career in Tech, and that's how I actually ended up in the engineering college in the first place. But, when I saw my cousins doing so well in their job in IT, that inspired me so much.[10]

Tara Ojo works as a software engineer at a large European online social learning platform. Unlike Bakshi, Ojo works on the front end, writing software code like HTML and JavaScript. She describes her day as 'working closely with other developers (on one computer) in a way that's really collaborative and allows a joined-up effort to build on learners' user experience'. Bakshi and Ojo, as female engineers, are a minority in a world where the number of software engineering positions are rising. Ojo explains, 'I'm grateful to have worked with lots of amazing women in the tech industry, but it is nowhere near equal and needs to be improved. At university there were about 3 women in a group of 20—and that ratio was the same across the other computer science subjects too.'[11]

---

[9] Krysten Crawford. 'A low-cost, scalable way to get more women into tech'. *Forbes India*. August 2023.

[10] 'Moneysupermarket – Swapna Bakshi, Mobile App tester'. *Women in Tech*.

[11] 'FutureLearn–Tara Ojo, Software Engineer'. *Women in Tech*.

The World Bank estimates that the global labour force participation rate for women is just over 50 per cent compared to 80 per cent for men.[12] Yet, as the global digital economy intensifies, new jobs are being created. The World Economic Forum estimated that 97 million new jobs will emerge by 2025, with a majority requiring skills in AI, engineering, product development, and emerging programming languages. However, despite the surging demand for these specialists, women have remained an untapped resource and are underrepresented. For example, women make up less than 25 per cent of people working as AI specialists.[13] In fact, the very roles where women have the lowest share of representation are exactly those that will have the highest demand and impact in coming years. These are roles related to data, cybersecurity, cloud computing, and app development. Surprisingly, the percentage of female STEM graduates entering into STEM employment is increasing, but after one year these graduates end up leaving. This trend seems to play out in many different countries including Singapore and Thailand.

Not employing women is a missed opportunity to tackle a talent shortage, which has been reported to cost the US over $160 billion, and nearly $45 billion in China in 2020.[14] Companies also lose out as a diverse workforce can increase productivity and revenues. When women represent more than 20 per cent of a company's management team, research shows that companies have approximately 10 per cent higher innovation revenues.[15] However, in large tech companies, women comprise just 25 per cent of their workforce. Even more worrying is that women who are already

[12] 'Female labour force participation'. *World Bank*. January 2022.

[13] *World Economic Forum Report 2020*.

[14] Ming En Liew and Yeo Zong Hao. 'Singapore's novel approaches to bridging the digital talent gap'. *Gov Insider*. July 2023.

[15] Vaishali Rastogi, Michael Meyer, Michael Tan, and Justine Tasiaux. 'Boosting Women in Technology in Southeast Asia'. October 2020.

in tech-related roles are leaving with many being put off by male dominated environments, in particular the 'bro culture'. That is, a culture of young, brash, (generally white) hyper-competitive men which can involve harassing women.[16] Despite the work being intellectually stimulating, women are dropping out of their tech jobs at a 45 per cent higher rate than men. Lack of career advancement and mentoring support have been reported as some of the top reasons.

At the same time, there is a gender pay gap and there are numerous studies that estimate the size of the gap. One reports that women earn up to 28 per cent less than their male colleagues in the same tech roles and the gap is larger in small businesses where the gap is between 19–20 per cent.[17] In the UK, Google's report shows that women earn 83p an hour for every £1 each male earns, and women's average bonuses are 43 per cent lower than men. There are several factors that could affect the gender pay gap, such as working in different hierarchy positions, skills, and previous experience. However, for those who do have the same set of skills and experience, the gap is unclear.

Lastly, there is a missed opportunity to not just have more women in technical roles like software engineers but also in managerial roles to drive digital transformation, particularly in fast-growing industries like e-commerce and finance. In financial services, an industry with a high rate of digital transformation, only 5.6 per cent of all fintech CEOs are women.[18] Bakshi explains:

> Women think the IT means only coding and they have to come from an IT/technical background to become an IT professional. I have seen people who come from commerce

---

[16] Sarah Benstead. 'Bro culture: What it is and why it's still an issue'. *Breathe*. January 2024.

[17] *Women in Tech Survey Report 2019.*

[18] *Fintech Diversity Radar 2021.*

and other background but still do really well in IT. I agree that coming from an IT background (from studies point of view) definitely helps but I personally believe as long as you are willing to learn and have a passion for something you can do anything.[19]

Increasing the scope of female participation can deliver significant economic benefits. If Europe doubled the share of women in the digital workforce to about 45 per cent, or an estimated 3.9 million additional women by 2027, it could benefit from a GDP increase of as much as 280 billion to 647 billion.[20] In Australia, it is the same story. Malarndirri McCarthy, Assistant Minister for Indigenous Australians and Indigenous Health of Australia, highlighted that if the proportion of women in the digital workforce in her country increased, the economy would grow by $1.2 billion a year.[21] To achieve these targets, tailored, practical solutions are needed where everyone is involved. We will get to these solutions later in the book. First, we must be clear on where the opportunities lie.

Better Innovation for Women

'The quality, relevance, and impact of the products and services output by the technology sector can only be improved by

---

[19] 'Moneysupermarket – Swapna Bakshi, Mobile App tester'. *Women in Tech.*

[20] Sven Blumberg, Melanie Krawina, Elina Mäkelä, and Henning Soller. 'Women in tech: The best bet to solve Europe's talent shortage'. *McKinsey Digital.* January 2023.

[21] 'Australia's National Statement for the 67th Session of the United Nations Commission on the Status of Women'. *Australian Government, Department of Prime Minister and Cabinet.* March 2023. https://ministers.pmc.gov.au/mccarthy/2023/australias-national-statement-67th-session-united-nations-commission-status-women

having the people who are building them be demographically representative of the people who are using them.'[22]

            —Tracy Chou, software engineer, Pinterest

When Apple launched its health monitoring system, it boasted of being a comprehensive health app that tracks health indicators like blood pressure, number of steps taken, and the amount of alcohol in your blood. A year before the launch, Apple's senior vice president of software engineering, Craig Federighi, claimed that the app would let users 'monitor all of your metrics that you're most interested in'.[23] Unfortunately, soon after the CEO launched Apple Health in 2014, a number of women pointed out they had forgotten to include a period tracker. The women criticized how a health app could neglect one of the most important aspects of women's health. Since the complaint, the app has been redesigned and many other period trackers have been developed. Such issues could have been avoided if more women were involved in the design and development stages of the app.

    There are many examples of missed innovation, where opportunities to cater to women were forgotten. Some fitbit devices don't take into account common female activity like pushing a pram or housework, which is a burden that continues to fall on women. Fitness monitors were found to underestimate the number of steps taken during housework by up to 74 per cent, and so underestimated the calories burned by housework by 34 per cent.[24] Women have also complained that smartphones are too big and have been designed for male hands.

---

[22] Tracy Chou. 'Why I Care About Diversity in Tech'. April 2014.

[23] Rose Eveleth. 'How Self-Tracking Apps Exclude Women'. *The Atlantic*. December 2014. https://www.theatlantic.com/technology/archive/2014/12/how-self-tracking-apps-exclude-women/383673/

[24] Nelson, M.B., Kaminsky, L.A., Dickin, D.C., & Montoye, A.H. (2016). 'Validity of Consumer-Based Physical Activity Monitors for Specific Activity Types'. *Medicine and Science in Sports and Exercise*, 48 8, 1619-28 .

More women in the digital economy can boost innovation for women. Women should be included at every stage of the design process, especially testing products and services to provide feedback and to check that the products are functional and cater to women's needs and preferences. Take, for example, earphones. Michael Koss, CEO of Koss Stereophones, said that his two daughters, three sisters, and wife complained that earbuds were painful, and the sound quality was off because the devices did not fit their ears properly. Koss listened to the women in his life and the company spent two years designing Koss Fit, a new line of earbuds that were 30 per cent smaller and fitted comfortably inside women's ears. The new earphones were developed by a team of women that worked with gold medallist athlete Dara Torres. The Koss Fit Series received great reviews from women all around the globe.[25] Colourful FitClips and FitBuds designed by women made it easier for other women to listen to music on the move, during intense workouts, without having the inconvenience of having their earphones fall out.

Biased algorithms are another example of where innovation has let women down, resulting in a missed opportunity for AI to do good. Since 2014, Amazon started building computer programs to review job applications with the aim of mechanizing the search process for top talent.[26] The computer models were trained by looking at patterns in CVs submitted over the ten previous years. However, most of the CVs belonged to men, creating a machine-learned-bias that favoured male applicants. In China, a study found searching for words like 'CEO' or 'scientist' often returns images of men.[27] Algorithms have also been problematic

[25] 'Women Love the Fit Series'. *Koss*. December 2013.

[26] Jeffrey Dastin. 'Insight - Amazon scraps secret AI recruiting tool that showed bias against women'. *Reuters*. October 2018. https://www.reuters.com/article/us-amazon-com-jobs-automation-insight-idUSKCN1MK08G

[27] Phoebe Zhang. 'The 'CEO' is a man: how Chinese artificial intelligence perpetuates gender biases'. *South China Morning Post*. September 2021.

in face and voice recognition software as there are examples where they failed to accurately detect women's faces and voices. Joy Buolamwini at MIT tested three commercially available face-recognition systems, created by Microsoft, IBM, and the Chinese company Megvii. The systems correctly identified the gender of white men 99 per cent of the time. But the error rate rose for people with darker skin, reaching nearly 35 per cent for women.[28] Buolamwini's results were alarming, and the study was featured in a documentary to stress its importance. The film *Coded Bias* premiered at the 2020 Sundance Film Festival. Directed by Shalini Kantayya, an American filmmaker, the film highlights the lack of legal structures for AI causing AI technologies to discriminate by race and gender. The consequences are that when these AI tools are used to decide housing, career opportunities, healthcare, and credit and education services, non-white, non-male individuals could miss out. There is a missed opportunity to develop unbiased algorithms that benefit women from diverse backgrounds. Having women represented is an easy solution but not always adopted. For instance, in November 2023, OpenAI's board fired its CEO, Sam Altman, only to have him return days later with a newly appointed board. Two female board members, Helen Toner, AI safety researcher, and Tasha McCauley, a robotics engineer who leads a 3D-mapping startup, were fired, creating a significant gender imbalance among the company's governance board. You might say that board changes happen all the time, for whatever reason. That is true, but what is significant about this is that a global innovator, at the time of writing, has no women in its board room. OpenAI developed ChatGPT which reached 100 million users just two months after launching. The rate of growth was described as unprecedented for a consumer app, as many people signed up to see what it was

---

[28] Timothy Revell. 'Face-recognition software is perfect – if you're a white man'. *New Scientist.* February 2018.

all about. So, did this major AI app inventor forget to recruit women? Were there no women to take on the board role? Many leading female AI experts were named as possible candidates. According to a Bloomberg report, philanthropist Laurene Powell Jobs, former Yahoo CEO Marissa Mayer, and former US Secretary of State Condoleezza Rice were all considered but not selected. Some female experts were quick to come out to say that they were not interested. OpenAI realized it needs to take action. While it is reportedly planning to expand the board soon, the initial board change was a missed opportunity to include more women in the AI revolution.

An opportunity exists to ensure new emerging technologies don't forget to cater to women. One example is the development of driverless cars. In a study conducted by Newcastle University in the UK, researchers asked thirty-three female and forty-three male drivers to get behind the wheel of their DriveLAB simulator.[29] The participants were asked to read aloud from an iPad while in the driver's seat of the simulator. After one minute, the simulator notified them of a parked car blocking the way ahead, and requested they take over driving while it continued at its current speed. The participants then had twenty seconds to spot the obstacle, manoeuvre the vehicle to change lanes, and avoid a crash. The study found that women were quicker to respond, leading to a recommendation that self-driving cars may need to have gender-specific settings, as women are better than men at taking control of the vehicle when there is an emergency.[30] Drivers with a delayed response may need earlier warnings to take control of the self-driving car.

---

[29] Shuo Li, Phil Blythe, Yanghanzi Zhang, Simon Edwards, Weihong Guo, Yanjie Ji, Paul Goodman, Graeme Hill, and Anil Namdeo. 'Analysing the effect of gender on the human–machine interaction in level 3 automated vehicles'. *Scientific Reports 12, 11645*. July 2022.
[30] Ibid.

Better Investor Returns

'It's nonsense for investors to claim that there aren't any women entrepreneurs in fintech to invest in. Investors are simply not looking hard enough.'[31]

—Martha Mghendi-Fisher, founder, African Women in Fintech and Payments

In 2018, Silicon Valley Bank (SVB) published a report on Women in Technology Leadership.[32] The American bank, which provides financial services to the technology industry, highlighted that companies with at least one female founder found it more difficult than companies with only male founders to raise funds. The Bank was on a mission to change that and asked, 'What can we do differently?' The bank knew that women entrepreneurs were a massive market opportunity as women are generally underbanked or underserved by their bank. For female entrepreneurs the challenge of accessing finance is even harder. The World Bank reported that women are often excluded from formal banking due to the lack of official identification and access to mobile devices.[33] In some instances, cultural norms make it difficult for women-led businesses to gain access to finance. SVB recognized this challenge and saw a market opportunity. Karen Cahn, CEO of iFundWomen, a funding marketplace for women-led start-

---

[31] Nita Bhalla. 'Move over "tech bros": Women entrepreneurs join Africa's fintech boom'. *Reuters*. February 2022. https://www.reuters.com/article/africa-women-tech-idUSL4N2UI39V

[32] 'Women in Technology Leadership 2018. Key Insights from the Silicon Valley Bank Startup Outlook Survey'. *Silicon Valley Bank*.

[33] 'The Global Findex Database 2021'. *World Bank*.

ups and small businesses, said, 'they were very bullish on trying to engage with our community in various ways.'[34]

Soon, SVB became well known for their commitment to Diversity, Equity, and Inclusion (DEI) and was named in Bloomberg's gender equality index five times in a row.[35] In January 2023, the bank president and CEO, Greg Becker, said, 'We have a responsibility and a unique opportunity to ensure women and people of underrepresented groups can access, contribute to and benefit from the enormous potential of the innovation economy.'[36]

There is a growing body of evidence that suggests investing in women-led startups can be extremely profitable. A study by First Round Capital found that companies with a female founder performed 63 per cent better than those without.[37] Despite this evidence, women-led startups only receive around 3 per cent of all venture capital funding but generate 78 cents for every dollar of funding. Boston Consulting Group (BCG) estimates that investors could have earned an additional $85 million by investing in both male- and female-founded startups over a five-year period. This is a missed economic opportunity for investors to fund more women-led start-ups. While there has been some shift towards investing in women, there is still significant scope for more change.

When SVB collapsed in March 2023, it was described as the largest American bank failure since the 2008 financial crisis. The collapse induced shocks through the international financial system. There were also concerns that the bank's shut down would

---

[34] Chabeli Carrazana. 'Women and minority business owners relied on Silicon Valley Bank when other banks turned them away. Now what?' *The 19th*. March 2023.

[35] 'SVB Included in Bloomberg Gender-Equality Index for Fifth Year'. *Silicon Valley Bank*. January 2023.

[36] Rebekah Bastian. 'The Silicon Valley Bank Collapse Disproportionately Impacts Underbanked Founders.' *Forbes*. March 2023.

[37] First Round 10 Year Project. https://10years.firstround.com/

have a disproportional impact on the women-led companies that it supported. Where would female founders go for credit? This, too, turned out to be a missed opportunity for other investors to come in and fill the gap. Female entrepreneurs tend to create innovative solutions to solving real world social problems.[38] As SVB found, women are more likely than men to start companies in underserved markets, such as healthcare and education, creating new markets and customer segments for investors. This explains the examples highlighted in earlier (and later) chapters about women starting their own businesses in edtuech, health-tech, climate-tech, and fintech.

However, a key issue is that most investors are men. If they have successfully invested in tech companies led by men, investors aim to repeat past successes and stay within their familiar networks. This puts women at a disadvantage as they can be seen as risky outsiders, especially in technology-based companies. Presently, only about 12 per cent of decision makers at venture capital firms are women, highlighting the need to get more women investors into decision-making positions.[39] For example, Female Founders Fund, founded by Anu Duggal, focuses on women-led companies in the e-commerce sector. Merian Ventures focuses on women-led companies, specifically in cybersecurity, blockchain, AI, and machine learning spaces. Jo Ann Corkran and Loretta McCarthy, the co-founders of Golden Seeds, highlighted: 'We're at a point where women have the highest level of education they've ever had and the

---

[38] Dr Ashlie L Burkart. 'Women entrepreneurs are a missed opportunity in venture capital. Here's how investors and policymakers can change that'. *AgFunder News*. June 2023.

[39] Dr Ashlie L Burkart, MD. 'Women entrepreneurs are a missed opportunity in venture capital. Here's how investors and policymakers can change that'. *AgFunder*. June 2023.

highest level of professional skills they've ever had.'[40] McCarthy says, 'They have the aptitude to run a business, so with proper funding there's no reason they can't do as well or better than companies run by men.'[41] Having more female investors can deliver higher returns. Female investors tend to outperform men by forty basis points.[42] Furthermore, women are more likely to invest in other women and so there is an opportunity for women to leverage their own networks for funding. All these efforts to increase investment in women-owned businesses has the potential to close the finance gaps estimated to be valued at $1.7 trillion.[43]

Better Policies and Regulation

> 'AI can be misused, or it can be used by bad actors. So then, there are questions about how you govern the use of this technology globally?'[44]
>
> —Mira Murati, CTO, OpenAI

Jenny was bullied when she was young. But this was not bullying in the classroom where she could look her bully in the eye, this was bullying while using the internet. Cyberbullying is harassment and intimidation that takes place online through digital devices. While social media platforms are the most common places for cyberbullying, harmful text messages, emails, or phone calls can also be used to bully someone.

---

[40] Michele Lerner. 'Future Returns: Angel Investing in Women-Led Companies'. *Barrons*. February 2023.

[41] Ibid.

[42] Kate Dore. 'Women investors are still outperforming men, study finds'. *CNBC*. October 2021.

[43] 'Micro-Small Medium Enterprises Finance Gap'. *World Bank, SME Forum, and International Finance Corporation*. 2017.

[44] John Simons. 'Mira Murati, The Creator of ChatGPT, Thinks AI Should Be Regulated.' *TIME*. February 2023.

Girls are more likely than boys to be both victims and perpetrators of cyberbullying. Nearly 15 per cent of teen girls have been the target of different kinds of abusive behaviour online compared with 6 per cent of boys. It is not just girls that are facing online abuse. A 2018 study by the Inter-Parliamentary Union in forty-five European countries found that over half of the women parliamentarians and parliamentary staff interviewed had experienced sexist attacks on social media, including repeated misogynistic insults and incitement to hatred, nude photomontages, and pornographic videos.[45] Female entrepreneurs are suffering too. Around 47 per cent of female entrepreneurs in developing countries reported online harassment, threats, and stalking. These threats can cause significant economic damage in the form of lost work and higher health care costs.[46]

To increase participation in the digital economy, it is important to provide a safe environment for women and girls. One important way is for legal frameworks and regulations to promote internet safety for women. Countries like Ireland have already passed new legislation that enforces online safety, with Singapore and the UK proposing similar legislation. Australia was the first country to take such action. In 2014, the New Zealand and Australian celebrity, Charlotte Dawson, took her own life. As a television presenter, she shined the light on cyberbullying, which started a new wave of mental health struggles for her. Dawson was harassed online despite being ambassador of an anti-cyberbullying initiative called 'Community Brave'.[47] She

[45] 'Gender Equality Index 2020: Digitalisation and the future of work'. *European Institute for Gender Equality.* https://old.eige.europa.eu/publications/gender-equality-index-2020-report/gender-based-violence-enabled-digital-technology-new-occupational-hazard

[46] 'The Urgent Case for Gender Equality in the Digital Age'. FP *Analytics, Foreign Policy.* https://fpanalytics.foreignpolicy.com/2021/05/13/the-urgent-case-for-gender-equality-in-the-digital-age/

[47] 'Charlotte Dawson hospitalised after troll war.' *New Zealand Herald Online.* August 2012.

fought back but this was just the start. She was later trolled on social media again when she made remarks on TV about the outfits worn by the partners of Australia's Rugby League footballers.[48] On 22 February 2014, Dawson died by suicide in her home in Sydney. This was the trigger for the Australian government to set up eSafety, an independent regulator for online safety. Julie Inman Grant, the eSafety commissioner, shared that she too had been exposed to online abuse that had been horrifically violent and misogynistic. However, as commissioner, she is proud of the small regulator protecting women while recognizing that more needs to be done as technology evolves:[49]

> [O]ur content removal powers are some of the most robust in the world, the online landscape is expanding and morphing at a rate that is impossible to compute. I'm concerned that new and emerging technologies, such as generative artificial intelligence and immersive tech, may be weaponised to cause further harm to women and girls in ways that are both more visceral, but also more difficult to detect. We need industry to proactively build in safety from the outset, rather than bolting it on when harm has occurred. This is fundamental to the Safety by Design approach.[50]

There is also a need for AI regulation to combat sexist algorithms which are going undetected. A global analysis of 133 AI systems from 1988 to today found that 44 per cent displayed gender bias, with 26 per cent exhibiting both gender and racial bias—leading to lower service quality, unequal resource distribution, and the reinforcement of harmful stereotypes. In the UK, given that

---

[48] Andrew Hornery. 'Dawson defends decision to out trolls'. *The Sydney Morning Herald*. October 2012.

[49] 'Meet Julie Inman Grant: Australia's Online Safety Commissioner on Protecting Women from Internet Abuse'. *Bumble*. June 2023. https://bumble.com/en/the-buzz/bumble-australia-apac-esafety-online-safety-julie-inman-grant

[50] Ibid.

women felt less confident about their online safety than men, despite spending a quarter of their day online, the regulator pushed for women's voices to be heard. Melanie Dawes from the UK media regulator said, 'We urge tech companies to take women's online safety concerns seriously and place people's safety at the heart of their services. That includes listening to feedback from users when they design their services and the algorithms that serve up content.'[51] Dawes explained that 'Some of the worst harms are caused, not so much by individual posts, but actually when things go viral and are shared with hundreds of thousands of people.'[52]

AI regulation is currently being debated all over the world. Europe has been leading the way as the parliament's priority is to make sure that AI systems used in the EU are safe, transparent, traceable, non-discriminatory, and environmentally friendly. Its aim is to ensure that AI systems are overseen by people, rather than by automation, to prevent harmful outcomes. Carlien Scheele, director of the European Institute for Gender Equality, supports the European legislation, saying that it can help women pursue their career ambitions through reducing AI discrimination. She says that measures such as the AI Act can tackle biases and discrimination in the short term, but that boosting female representation in AI over the long term is equally important. Scheele commented that women make up over half of Europe's population, but only 16 per cent of its AI workers.[53] She says that until AI reflects the diversity of society, it 'will cause more problems than it solves', adding that 'in AI, limited representation

[51] Natasha Lomas. 'Social media giants are failing women, finds Ofcom'. *TechCrunch* https://techcrunch.com/2022/06/01/ofcom-women-online-nation-2022-report/

[52] Natasha Lomas. 'Social media giants are failing women, finds Ofcom'. *TechCrunch*. June 2022. https://techcrunch.com/2022/06/01/ofcom-women-online-nation-2022-report/

[53] Carlien Scheele. 'Artificial intelligence and gender equality.' *European Institute for Gender Equality*. April 2022.

leads to the creation of datasets with inbuilt biases that can perpetuate stereotypes about gender'.[54] There is an opportunity for female policymakers and global leaders to represent female voices in the design of AI regulation and governance. More women in senior government can advance this change. There is growing evidence that women's leadership in political decision-making processes improves the quality of the decisions and advancement of gender equality.[55] Unfortunately, latest data shows that women constitute only 22 per cent of cabinet members that are heading government ministries responsible for leading policy change. Only thirteen countries have 50 per cent or more women holding cabinet positions.[56]

India has announced that it will follow Rwanda in applying quotas to boost the number of women holding political office. In 2003, Rwanda set a 30 per cent quota for women in elected positions, and it now has the highest share of women in any parliament around the world, at 61 per cent.[57] Clare Akamanzi, CEO of the Rwanda Development Board, stated: 'Deliberate leadership for gender inclusion is important. My president will make sure when he's appointing cabinet, women are represented.'[58] New Zealand and Mexico are other countries that have a high female representation in parliament. Mexico's parliament achieved gender parity in 2018, and New Zealand has had three female prime ministers.[59] Christine Lagarde, the head of IMF, says, 'Representation shapes policy. Diversity leads to better quality

[54] Ibid.

[55] 'Descriptive representation: Policy outcomes and municipal day-care coverage in Norway'. *American Journal of Political Science*, 46(2), pp. 428–37.

[56] 'Women in Politics: 2023'. *Inter-Parliamentary Union and UN Women.*

[57] 'Revisiting Rwanda five years after record-breaking parliamentary elections'. *UN Women.* August 2018.

[58] Ian Shine. 'This is what countries are doing to get more women into positions of power.' *World Economic Forum.* October 2023.

[59] 'Mexican Parliament achieves gender parity'. *Inter-Parliamentary Union.* July 2018.

decision-making.'[60] In her opinion, there might not have been a financial crisis if we'd had more women on boards.

The Gender Equality Action Coalition on Technology and Innovation for Gender Equality, organized by the UN and Mexican and French governments, is trying to increase female representation. The coalition includes the governments of Finland, Chile, Tunisia, Armenia and Rwanda, and companies like Microsoft and Salesforce as well as other multinational institutions. All stakeholders have agreed to fast-track women's tech leadership and support the entry of women and girls in technology roles. With diversity around AI becoming a key concern, could quotas on AI organizations be the answer?

What are the missed opportunities for women?

There is a digital revolution and a female revolution. But they are happening at a different pace leading to missed opportunities in terms of innovation (by women for women), careers for women, policies to protect girls and women from cyberbullying, biased algorithms, and missed opportunities to invest in the women courageous enough to lead social, digital, and economic transformations. Failure to take action can come at a huge economic and social cost. The opportunities can be realized by government, investors, and businesses taking action. In the next chapter, we attempt to explain what is at stake and how each agent can play a part to make sure that women don't lose out.

---

[60] Richard Partington. "'If it was Lehman Sisters, it would be a different world" – Christine Lagarde'. *The Guardian*. September 2018.

Chapter 4

Female Digital Economic Agents

'Women should no longer be thought of as a niche. In fact, they're one of the most significant growth markets we've ever seen.'[1]

—Monique Woodard, managing director, Cake Ventures

Over the past twenty years, there have been constantly more men than women living on the planet. Believe it or not, most countries and regions in the world have more women than men.[2] The two most populous countries—China and India, which are also two big tech nations—have a higher male population. But if we exclude them, there are more women in the world. Furthermore, these women are creating significant economic impact. In the US, that impact was estimated to be $8.95 billion in 2023. Some are describing this as a financial boom. 'When it comes to incremental impact, women have caused a 0.5% GDP "bump" in the US GDP–more revenue than the 2008 Olympics,' says Julie Yufe,

---

[1] Monique Woodard. 'Unlocking the trillion-dollar female economy'. *TechCrunch*. May 2023.

[2] 'World sex ratio 2024'. *StatisticsTimes*. https://statisticstimes.com/demographics/world-sex-ratio.php

World Bank. https://data.worldbank.org/indicator/SP.POP.TOTL.FE.ZS

SVP Vodka & Rum at Diageo.[3] By 2028, women will account for 75 per cent of all discretionary spending; that is, expenses such as dining out, hobbies, travel, and personal care. Journalist Brittany Jones-Cooper is calling it 'the great wealth transfer' as 'women are going to be holding the purse strings in 20 to 30 years'.

Despite this, as we learned in the previous chapter, women remain significantly underrepresented in all aspects of the growing global digital economy. There is an opportunity to increase their digital participation and think of women as powerful economic agents. As individuals, they are large consumers of high-end, high-value goods. As business owners or leaders, women are using their collaborative skills to boost sales and earn profits, often catering to women. In the government, they are delivering better welfare services to vulnerable groups including children, senior women, and mothers. Taken together, there is a multiplier effect throughout the economy. Take, for example, FIFA Women's World Cup Football. The 2023 games hosted by Australia and New Zealand increased interest in the women's game along with boosting the economy. Airwallex ANZ general manager, Luke Latham, said that 'The world game is living up to its name with our tracker showing international visitors have so far spent an extra $2.99 billion at Australian hotels and retailers.'[4] The football games gained global attention with increased viewers from Asia, the Middle East, North Africa, Europe, and Latin America, attracting more businesses to get involved. The match against Australia and England had one of the biggest audiences.

---

[3] 'Women are causing a financial boom. What's fueling the "Sheconomy"?' *The Female Quotient. IMD*. October 2023. https://www.imd.org/ibyimd/leadership/women-are-causing-a-financial-boom-whats-fueling-the-sheconomy/

[4] Theodore Koumelis.'World Cup gives $3 billion boost to NSW visitor economy.' *Travel Daily News*. August 2023.

It was attended by 75,784 people, with 11.15 million watching on TV.[5] After the England win the number of google searches for 'flights to Australia' shot up by 179 per cent. The hospitality sector also signed its first partnership between FIFA Women's World Cup 2023 and Booking.com. It is anticipated that the games could generate as much as $300 million and $40 million for Australia and New Zealand respectively. This is more than the $200 million generated from the women's games in France in 2019.[6] The visibility and influence of female footballers extends beyond the game, as they leverage their platforms to advocate for gender equality, inclusivity, and social progress. This advocacy resonates with courageous women in technology who strive to create more equitable workplaces and challenge biases within the industry.

In this stage of the journey, we invite you to start thinking of women as powerful digital economic agents shaping our economy. We provide examples from China, the US, Latin America, Europe, Africa, and the Middle East to show women's role as digital consumers, digital businesses, digital entrepreneurs, digital business owners or leaders, as well as digital government. The international examples highlight that the economic influence of women is not isolated to one specific industry or geographic region or public or private sector. While every country has different gender issues, driven by different social, political, and economic policies, fearless women, regardless of their race, ethnicity, or profession, are taking it upon themselves to make a difference.

---

[5] Ibid

[6] Kevin Tjoe. '5 ways tour and activity operators can make the most of the 2023 FIFA Women's World Cup'. *Rezdy*. January 2023.

Female Digital Consumers

'I think what we're seeing right now is that women are not to be underestimated. They lift up economies and that impact is not to be overlooked.'[7]

—Kristina Chiappetta, executive strategy director,
Landor & Fitch

Women control an estimated $20 trillion in annual consumer spending worldwide.[8] With greater employment opportunities and higher income jobs, combined with a greater push for digital and financial inclusion, more women are shopping online. This means higher consumption from a 'digital customer' either on websites, mobile apps, or on social media. In Southeast Asia, women are driving the growth of online shopping in the region, with many preferring it to the offline mode. Around 63 per cent of the women browse the internet at least once a day for products and services, with nearly 30 per cent doing so twice or more per day. Further, just under 80 per cent of women in the region buy groceries online.

On a global basis, nearly 50 per cent of all female shoppers buy clothes and shoes over the internet and this trend is driving online fashion, generating almost $1 trillion in revenue in 2023. Brands like Skims, SHEIN, and Savage x Fenty are creating a multiplier effect as they attract new consumer brands and activity from creators and influencers, as well as supply chain companies benefitting from the rise in e-commerce.[9] In the Asia-Pacific,

---

[7] Vanessa Yurkevich. 'Taylor Swift, Barbie and Beyoncé are unleashing the spending power of women'. *CNN*. August 2023. https://edition.cnn.com/2023/08/09/economy/barbie-taylor-swift-beyonce-economic-impact/index.html

[8] Michael J. Silverstein and Kate Sayre. 'The Female Economy'. *Harvard Business Review*. 2009.

[9] Monique Woodard. 'Unlocking the trillion-dollar female economy'. *TechCrunch*. May 2023.

McKinsey estimates that if women's economic empowerment were to play out to its full potential, it could deliver as much as one-fifth of additional consumption growth in Asia.[10]

Currently, China has one of the highest women's labour force participation and full-time employment rates in the Asia-Pacific. It is estimated that 97 per cent of urban Chinese women have an income. Women are increasingly populating Chinese tech offices as China's biggest internet companies have at least 40 per cent female staff. Women are studying more as female graduates from tertiary education centres outnumber their male peers.[11] By studying more and working more, the country's consumption is being driven by financially independent young women, particularly those from the millennial and Gen-Z generations.[12] In 2018, women accounted for 55 per cent of online spending, significantly more than their proportion of the population. Economics professor Qiu Xiaodong at Beijing's Jiaotong University said that 'The new generation, girls born in the '80s and '90s, live in a time when the country's economy is growing, their income is growing, and then their parents' consumption power and consumption concept are changing.'[13] With the rising income, there is also an increase in wealth. China is home to nearly 400 million female consumers aged twenty to sixty, who account for as much as $1.9 trillion in spending annually.

---

[10] Oliver Tonby, Jonathan Woetzel, Rohit Razdan, Wonsik Choi, Naomi Yamakawa, Jeongmin Seong, and Tiago Devesa. 'The trailblazing consumers in Asia propelling growth'. *McKinsey Global Institute.* June 2021.

[11] Glyn Atwal. 'The Rise of China's Alpha Women'. *Jing Daily.* December 2021. https://jingdaily.com/the-rise-of-chinas-alpha-women/

[12] Ashley Dudarenok. 'Winning Over The "She Economy": How to Tap Female Consumption In China'. *Jing Daily.* March 2023. https://jingdaily.com/china-she-economy-female-consumption/

[13] Dawn Lui. 'China's $670 billion "sheconomy" is growing like crazy.' *NBC News.* May 2019.

China's digital economy is an important driver of the country's growth. In 2022, its digital economy exceeded $9.5 trillion and it has plans to continue expanding and innovating.[14] China's 'she economy' is expected to continue growing too, despite China having 31.6 million more males than females in 2018.[15] Mobile shopping has become the norm for Chinese female internet users. As of February 2020, China recorded nearly 450 million female mobile shoppers. Compared to male shoppers, female consumers are more willing to participate in online shopping events and embracing new features like social commerce and live streaming commerce.[16] Take, for example, International Women's Day. Every year, China marks the day with a festival of celebrations. But it is also known as a national shopping holiday described as Goddess Day or Queens Day, as every major e-commerce platform holds sales promotions targeting women. In 2022, Tmall, the platform for local Chinese and international brands, successfully curated a presale on the first night of celebrations with a famous live streamer Li Jiaqi, known as the 'Lipstick Brother'.[17] The event saw over 70 million tune into Li's live streaming room where a total of 279 products were on offer. That night online sales reached $3915 million. Female digital customers are having a significant economic effect.

Fiona Yang, a thirty-four-year-old teacher living in Beijing frequently shops online says:

---

[14] 'China's Digital Economy Exceeds 50 Trillion Yuan'. *China Daily*. May 2023.

[15] Dawn Liu. 'China's $670 billion "sheconomy" is growing like crazy'. *CNBC*. May 2019. https://www.cnbc.com/2019/05/03/chinas-670-billion-sheconomy-is-growing-like-crazy.html

[16] 'Frequency of online purchases in China as of June 2022, by gender'. *Statista*.

[17] 'Li Jiaqi hits record high sales as Tmall's Women's Day Festival kicks off'. *Dao Insights*. June 2022. https://daoinsights.com/news/li-jiaqi-hits-record-high-sales-as-tmalls-womens-day-festival-kicks-off/

I don't shop around. It's too time-consuming. That's why I really just use Taobao. It gives me a headache doing lengthy comparisons. I prefer to have options because I want to see different styles and prices, but overall I prefer just to buy from a platform I trust and know than shop around for the cheapest products. What I like about the way Taobao functions is that once you see a product you like and click 'Like', when you go back to the previous page, Taobao automatically shows you options for the same product (so you don't need to search again) and makes it super easy to do your own price comparison. It takes so little effort. Then, you can just focus on the reviews rather than the price.[18]

There are many more like Yang. In 2021, around 17.8 percent of female consumers spent more than $141 (¥1,000) online, showing a slight increase from the same period in the previous year.[19] In June 2022, about 74 per cent of the female respondents said they had made online purchases at least once a week.[20] It's no surprise that China is estimated to be the world's third-largest consumer market for women, equivalent to the combined retail markets of Germany, France, and the UK.

Digital Businesses

'The world is starving for new ideas and great leaders who will champion those ideas.'[21]

—Lisa Su, CEO, Advanced Micro Devices

---

[18] 'How Chinese women really shop: 4 case studies'. *Focus*. June 2023.

[19] 'Online spending level of female consumers in China as of January 2021'. *Statista*.

[20] 'Frequency of online purchases in China as of June 2022, by gender'. *Statista*.

[21] 'Thirty of the most compelling leadership quotes by women.' *The CEO Magazine*. April 2023.

Digital technologies are bringing about a new way of doing business. Digital business transformation is changing how products and services are delivered and traditional businesses are forced to innovate to stay ahead of the competition. Business leaders need to know how to use digital tools effectively to inform decision making and improve customer products, services, and experiences. In this regard, women are seizing opportunities to take up digital leadership positions to successfully lead companies with their creative, solution-orientated approach.

One major industry that has been digitally disrupted is banking. Traditional banks are facing competition from digital-only banks, also known as neobanks. These banks operate entirely online and offer customers a range of digital services, including mobile banking, budgeting tools, and instant money transfers. The largest neobank in the world is Nubank and its co-founder, Cristina Junqueira, is one of the most successful female fintech entrepreneurs in Latin America. With a background in engineering, Junqueira made her way through management consulting and landed a job supervising a credit card portfolio at one of Brazil's largest banks. Hoping to change the industry, Junqueira helped Nubank develop a user-friendly digital financial app, which is one of the largest digital-banking platforms in the world with more than 53 million customers across Latin America.[22] During the bank's growth, Junqueira gave birth to three daughters and has been a supporter of gender inclusion in the workplace. Her contribution to the fintech industry and female empowerment in entrepreneurship has been recognized by Fortune's 40 Under 40 list.

---

[22] Laura Furstenthal, Dinah Hanson, Risha Kaushal, Katie Lelarge, Tiffany Qiang, and Paige Xu. 'The Committed Innovator: Women continuing to change the world'. *McKinsey & Company*. March 2022. https://www.mckinsey.com/capabilities/strategy-and-corporate-finance/our-insights/women-innovators

Over the decade, technological development has also led to large tech businesses, now known as Big Tech. The ten largest tech companies by market capitalization are Apple, Microsoft, Google, Amazon, Nvidia, Tesla, Meta, TSMC, Tencent, and Broadcom. Among the top twenty is Advanced Micro Devices (AMD), an American chip developer headquartered in Santa Clara, California. AMD develops and produces microprocessors, chipsets, graphics chips, and system-on-chip. These products may not sound glamourous, but they are essential for the digital economy. They are at the heart of the devices that we use to work, travel, stay fit, and entertain ourselves—from cars to smartphones, and from MRI scanners to industrial robots and data centres. With the rising deployment of AI, the demand for chips is soaring.

One of AMD's fiercest competitor's is Nvidia—an American company founded by a group of men, who are tailoring their chips to AI tasks. AMD is looking to compete against Nvidia in the AI revolution and its CEO is keen to win. Lisa Su is AMD's powerful CEO. She was appointed CEO in 2014 and since then the company's stock soared nearly thirty-fold.[23] As of 2023, Su had an estimated net worth of more than $700 million. As the daughter of a mathematician and a bookkeeper turned entrepreneur, Su was born in Taiwan, in 1969, and immigrated to New York City when she was just three years old.

When women like Su and Junqueira lead companies, research shows that there are positive knock-on effects felt throughout their organizations. Women are more likely than men to hire women, which means more female representation at C-suite level, leading to greater representation at every level. Women at the top of a company are also likely to create a healthier workplace culture (for both women and men alike). In the case of AMD, at the start

---

[23] 'Lisa Su.' *Forbes Profile*. https://www.forbes.com/profile/lisa-su/

of 2023 it appointed CFO Jean Hu from Marvell Technology, increasing diversity at the top.[24]

Digital transformation has become so vital for success in the digital economy that even traditional companies are changing. Coca-Cola is a brand that has been around since the second industrial revolution. In 1886, Atlanta, Georgia, Dr John Pemberton, a local pharmacist, produced the syrup for Coca-Cola and added carbonated water to make the drink.[25] Since then, the global beverage company serves its drinks in more than 200 countries and territories each day. With large distribution channels, Coca-Cola was keen to digitalize to become more efficient but found it needed to train its workforce. In 2022, it established a digital academy to upskill managers and frontline team leaders across its business operations.[26] In its first year, the academy trained more than 500 people in digital skills and boosted productivity and throughput by more than 20 per cent.[27]

Women are also leading innovation in traditional sectors like car manufacturing. From manual cars to self-driving cars, women have played a significant role in the car industry. For instance, in the 1920s, Dorothée Pullinger managed car production at the manufacturing company Galloway in Scotland.[28] Pullinger, who was a trained engineer, developed the Galloway car, a car made by women in southwest Scotland for women. The factory owned by Pullinger's father was originally built during the war to manufacture aeroplane parts, but Dorothée persuaded her father

---

[24] Wallace Witkowski. 'AMD is Making History for Asian Women Executives'. *Market Watch*. June 2023.

[25] Coca-Cola website: https://www.coca-cola.com/

[26] Daphne Luchtenberg and Roberto Migliorini. 'Coca-Cola: The people-first story of a digital transformation'. *McKinsey & company*. July 2022.

[27] Ibid.

[28] Graham Fraser. 'Dorothée Pullinger: "The pioneer who built a car for women, by women"'. *BBC*. June 2019.

to keep it open as a car factory and provide employment to many local women. Pullinger helped design the Galloway car, which was much smaller, to suit women. On some models, gears were placed in the middle, the seat was raised, storage space was added, the dashboard was lowered, and the steering wheel was smaller. Decades later, women are now shaping the AI revolution by innovating autonomous vehicles. A leading expert for these new generation of cars is Raquel Urtasun, a professor at the University of Toronto. In May 2017, the ride hailing platform Uber hired Urtasun to lead a Toronto-based research team on self-driving cars. She led a research group and hired dozens of researchers. In 2021, Urtasun left Uber and launched Waabi Innovation, focused on developing self-driving cars. 'Self-driving is one of the most exciting and important technologies of our generation. Once solved at scale, it will change the world as we know it,' says Urtasun.[29] Her company first launched a simulator to train and test the technology. It then introduced the Waabi Driver, which is an autonomous truck. 'Some of our competitors were very surprised. Then Volvo came along, and it was like, "Oh, my God, they really mean business."'[30]

Digital Entrepreneurs

'Access to technology is democratising the participation of women micropreneurs in the retail landscape today.'

—Pankaj Jathar, vice president and country head for India, Etsy[31]

---

[29] Waabi website: https://waabi.ai/

[30] Alex Mlynek. 'Why self-driving pioneer Raquel Urtasun is determined to solve our supply chain woes'. *The Globe and Mail*. March 2023.

[31] Madanmohan Rao. '"Connected women are key to a country's economic growth" – 20 quotes of the week on digital transformation'. *Your Story*. October 2022. https://yourstory.com/2022/10/connected-women-quotes-digital-transformation-economy-indian-startups

Warungs are small, family-owned businesses found in Indonesia. It's a place where you can hang out, eat, and buy snacks. The term 'warung' means a sense of familiarity and simplicity, emphasizing a welcoming and relaxing environment. Some warungs operate as mini convenience stores selling essential groceries and household items. It is common to find women managing warungs—cooking, serving customers, and managing finances. These local businesses make a significant economic contribution to Indonesian communities. A total of 65 million micro, small, and medium enterprises (MSMEs) in Indonesia contribute more than 61 per cent of the country's GDP. Women-owned MSMEs are a big part of that contribution. In 2021, around 65 per cent of all MSMEs (which could have fewer than four employees) were women-owned. It is expected that this percentage will increase as women continue to be empowered and entrepreneurial. In 2022, a Global Entrepreneurship study found that out of forty-nine countries, Indonesia was among the top four where there were more female entrepreneurs than men. Other studies show that Indonesian women are more active than men in high-growth businesses with innovative products and a strong international-market focus.[32]

A number of companies and government initiatives are assisting these women scale up their entrepreneurial ideas. In particular, homegrown digital platforms like Gojek, Tokopedia, and Bukalapak are providing digital solutions to allow female businesses to expand their reach.[33] For example, five years ago, Nova Mathovani created a café where young Indonesians could enjoy drinking jamu, a traditional Indonesian drink. Jamu—a

---

[32] *Global Entrepreneurship Monitor Report 2021.*

[33] 'Gojek's technology and innovation help women MSME players leverage businesses'. *The Jakarta Post.* December 2020. https://www.thejakartapost.com/ms/gojek-2019/2020/12/15/gojeks-technology-and-innovation-help-women-msme-players-leverage-businesses.html

drink made from natural ingredients including ginger, turmeric, and honey used as a remedy to colds, aches, and pains—was not very popular with the younger generation due to its smell and bitter taste.

Mathovani figured out how to make it cool, like drinking coffee in cafés, where the experience of drinking coffee is just as important as the taste. She found that there was a greater desire for healthy beverages and young people were curious about the drink. Together with her husband she opened Suwe Ora Jamu, a shop that serves different varieties of Jamu. Today, Mathovani has expanded into different parts of Jakarta. A key success factor in expanding her business was digitalization. She uses digital tools to coordinate operations and communicate with staff, suppliers, and customers more effectively. She also checks new products and orders samples from suppliers online instead of visiting in person. Mathovani's advice is that 'If there was a time machine to go back 5 years, I would do everything to prepare myself for the digital era. I feel that it is the right time to start a business because everything is so easy now. With just one click we can connect to many things.'[34]

Indonesia provides an example of how digital entrepreneurship can be a powerful avenue for women's inclusion in the digital economy. A digital entrepreneur is a business owner who runs their company online. Podcasters, bloggers, digital retailers, online course creators, and some types of freelancers, such as virtual assistants and graphic designers, are a few examples of digital entrepreneurs.

Another example of digital technology assisting female entrepreneurs is online platforms for buying and selling goods. E-commerce offers many women, especially in developing

---

[34] 'Keeping the jamu tradition alive'. *Women Will Indonesia*. https://senaillat.com/womenwill-indonesia

economies, a path to digital entrepreneurship that will boost household income. First, it offers lower entry barriers than traditional brick-and-mortar businesses. Women entrepreneurs can start their businesses with lower start-up costs and without the need for a physical storefront. Yvette Uwimpaye, a young entrepreneur from Rwanda, noticed the inconvenience people faced while shopping at multiple markets. To address this issue, she developed Murukali, a simplified online shopping platform that saves time and money. Uwimpaye explains, 'I became interested in how to combine business and Information Communication Technology (ICT) to provide product price information and how to easily access these products without physically moving around.'[35] With start-up costs as little as $1,155, she managed to launch the platform that is transforming the shopping experience in Rwanda. Second, e-commerce enables women entrepreneurs to reach customers globally. Birame Sock, an entrepreneur from Senegal, has taken advantage of this opportunity as founder of Kwely, an online Business-to-Business wholesale sourcing marketplace for products made in Africa. The company focuses on the development of existing and new Made-in-Africa brands and supports these local suppliers export overseas.[36]

As mentioned before, all over the world, female start-ups are springing up in a wide range of sectors, from health-tech to edutech, climate-tech, and fintech. For example, Davida Herzl, CEO and co-founder at Aclima, developed a new way to map and analyse air pollution and greenhouse gases. Aclima answers key questions about what's happening in the neighbourhood, where pollution levels are highest, who is being impacted, and where can

---

[35] Oluwabusayomi Sotunde. 'Trailblazing online shopping in Rwanda. How We Made it in Africa'. June 2018. https://www.howwemadeitinafrica.com/trailblazing-online-shopping-in-rwanda/61639/

[36] 'Birame Sock'. *Cartier Women's Initiative*. https://www.cartierwomensinitiative.com/jury/birame-sock

decision-makers target action to reduce emissions and protect public health. The Aclima app provides a new level of access and visibility for all stakeholders.

Digital entrepreneurship can also be found in the healthcare sector. Jenny Derfler, the CEO of Air Doctor, helps travellers find a doctor while abroad. Her platform enables travellers to schedule an appointment with any doctor in Europe, Asia, Australia, and the US. In fact, the Air Doctor was born precisely because Derfler went through this exact trouble of finding a doctor. A few years ago, Derfler found herself ill during a holiday in Budapest. Being in a foreign country, she faced the challenge of finding a private doctor who could assist her. Derfler explains:

> I realised the immense challenges that travellers face when seeking quality healthcare abroad, and how insurance processes can often add additional burdens to an already stressful situation . . . By leveraging technological advancements, data analytics, and a customer-centric approach, I believe that we can revolutionise the travel insurance sector.[37]

In relation to finance, in Africa, the average rate of women-led fintech has doubled. One example of the success is Okra, which launched in 2020. The company, founded by software engineer Fara Ashiru Jituboh, has built an open finance platform that enables developers and businesses to build personalized digital services and fintech products for customers.[38] 'Essentially, we

---

[37] 'STARTUP STORY: Jenny Cohen Derfler, CEO of Air Doctor, Talks Health and Travel'. *InsureTech Insights*. https://www.insurtechinsights.com/startup-story-jenny-cohen-derfler-ceo-of-air-doctor-talks-health-and-travel/

[38] Nita Bhalla. 'Move over 'tech bros': Women entrepreneurs join Africa's fintech boom'. *Women Entrepeneurs Finance Initiative*. https://we-fi.org/move-over-tech-bros-women-entrepreneurs-join-africas-fintech-boom/

play the "middleman" by enabling individuals and businesses to connect their bank accounts directly with third-party applications in real-time,' said Jituboh. Two years later, the startup has attracted 400 clients, including twenty banks in Nigeria, Kenya, and South Africa.

Huda Kattan, an American entrepreneur, makeup artist, and beauty blogger is a successful digital content creator. As an influencer, Kattan, like millions of other female influencers, monetizes her blogs, YouTube channels, podcasts, and social media accounts through advertising, sponsorships, and merchandise sales. It is estimated that around 84 per cent of influencers creating sponsored content are women and only 16 per cent are men. Kattan has over 50 million followers on Instagram.[39] With a net worth of $560 million, Kattan earned her fortune as the founder of the cosmetics line Huda Beauty.

Female digital entrepreneurship contributes to economic growth, innovation, and job creation. A study found that equal gender representation in business can increase profitability and productivity by 40 per cent.[40] The most notable characteristic of women entrepreneurs is that they tend to not only pursue economic gain, but also strive to make a positive social impact through their enterprises. When women are involved in community leadership, more money is reinvested in their local communities and filtered into education, childcare, and other local infrastructure needs.[41] This applies to women in the

---

[39] 'Huda Kattan Net Worth $560 Million'. *Celebrity Net Worth*. October 2023. https://www.celebritynetworth.com/richest-businessmen/business-executives/huda-kattan-net-worth/

[40] Mark Muckerheide. 'The finance gap for women entrepreneurs is $1.7 trillion. Here's how to close it.' *The World Economic Forum*. October 2023.

[41] 'In India, women's representation in local government councils, known as panchayats, has led to an average implementation of 62% more drinking water projects than in areas without female representation. In Norway, women's involvement in municipal councils resulted in better childcare facilities.'

digital economy. However, as we discovered earlier with the collapse of the bank SVB, female entrepreneurs often face unique challenges and barriers such as access to funding, gender bias, and a lack of networking opportunities. The countries with the best ecosystems for female founders—which include the US, Malaysia, China, and Australia—provide greater institutional support for SMEs, more positive sociocultural mindsets, and a higher willingness to take calculated risks.[42]

Digital Government

'I want a digitalised world that is inclusive, humane and fair. A digital economy that is innovative, open, entrepreneurial, resilient and safe.'[43]

—Alexandra van Huffelen, minister for digitalization,

Netherlands

Barcelona is a city rich with culture, art, and history. Overlooking the mediterranean sea, the city is famous for Antoni Gaudí's architecture, in particular the Sagrada Familia. In addition to its unique buildings, Barcelona is a smart city with a population of

---

R. Chattopadhyay and E. Duflo. 'Women as policy makers: Evidence from a randomized policy experiment in India'. *Econometrica* 72(5), pp. 1409–1443. 2004.

K. A. Bratton and L. P. Ray. 'Descriptive representation: Policy outcomes and municipal day-care coverage in Norway'. *American Journal of Political Science*, 46(2), pp. 428–437. 2002.

[42] 'The Mastercard Index of Women Entrepreneurs 2020 Report. Startup Genome Reveals Top 10 Startup Ecosystems for Female Founders'. *Startup Genome*. 2019.

[43] LinkedIn post by Alexandra van Huffelen 2023. https://www.linkedin.com/posts/alexandravanhuffelen_i-want-a-digitalized-world-that-is-inclusive-activity-7074275960551796737-KBjt?utm_source=share&utm_medium=member_desktop

around 5.7 million. The city uses IoT technology to effectively manage energy, waste, and water consumption as well as reduce noise. For example, the city has implemented smart meters and sensors in buildings to monitor and optimize energy usage, allowing for efficient energy management.

> Barcelona aims to create a new powerful vision where technology is an instrument to empower people and transform the city. In a truly democratic city, the citizens should be able to access knowledge commons, open data and the public information infrastructures of the city in order to have better and more affordable public services and a better quality of life.[44]

The person in charge of developing Barcelona's Digital City Plan is Francesca Bria. In 2018, Bria, as the chief technology and digital innovation officer of Barcelona City Council, implemented a plan with input from citizens, tech communities, policymakers, tech companies, and researchers. Bria's strategy was to look at how technology can serve the people of Barcelona. The plan outlines new directives, which establish the use of agile methods (a project management approach that prioritizes cross-functional collaboration and continuous improvement) for ICT projects. It also advocates for technological sovereignty (a political outlook where technology is aligned to the laws, needs and interests of the country in which users are located).[45] Such measures ensure control over data and information generated by digital technologies, and also public digital infrastructures based on free and open source software. The plan had some successes

---

[44] Barcelona Digital City.

[45] 'Government measure concerning ethical management and accountable data: Barcelona Data Commons.' Barcelona City Council Digital Plan. May 2018.

and Barcelona stands as a benchmark for smart policies that are deeply entrenched with digital social innovation.

Just like Barcelona, both local and central governments have been embarking on a digital journey to digitalize public services and public engagement with the government. Examples include online processes for paying government taxes or utilities, enrolling on social service programmes, or applying for birth certificates, marriage certificates and passports. To access these services, individuals need reliable internet access, a digital identity, and sufficient digital literacy to know how to download online forms, register details, and make online payments. Some e-government services are particularly important to women. For example, government websites with information on women's health and family planning, workplace rights, government programmes and services related to childcare, educational opportunities, and resources on legal aid. Sweden has a strong focus on gender equality and offers a wide range of e-government services that support women in various aspects of life, including healthcare, education, and entrepreneurship. Canada also has an extensive e-government infrastructure that includes resources and services aimed at supporting women's economic empowerment and safety.

The secret for success is having senior female representation within government. Having women in senior government positions is important to get women's voices heard. HE Huda AlHashimi, deputy minister of cabinet affairs for strategic affairs, the UAE[46] was involved in setting up the world's first government accelerator and the world's first virtual ministry. She considers her role as important as 'any government innovation strategy must draw on a diverse range of expertise from across society. It is vital,

---

[46] Yun Xuan Poon. 'HE Huda AlHashimi, Deputy Minister of Cabinet Affairs for Strategic Affairs, United Arab Emirates'. *GovInsider.* January 2022. https://govinsider.asia/intl-en/article/he-huda-alhashimi-deputy-minister-of-cabinet-affairs-for-strategic-affairs-united-arab-emirates-women-in-govtech-2021/

therefore, that governments engage not only women working in the public sector, but those in the private sector too, as well as women in society.'[47] AlHashimi is not the only powerful woman in government. The country's Sheikha Fatima, wife of Sheikh Zayed bin Sultan Al Nahyan—the founder and inaugural president of the UAE—launched a national strategy to support women in all aspects of their role as digital economic agents, increasing job opportunities to developing entrepreneurship skills for girls, homemakers, and female workers.[48]

In Taiwan, Hao-Ting Chang is a design consultant at the Public Digital Innovation Space.[49] When the pandemic broke out in Taiwan, in order to avoid a lack of public health supplies, Chang was involved in introducing tracked mask purchases at pharmacies with health insurance cards. Chang realized that there was a demand for 'knowing where there are surplus masks to buy' and came up with the idea of sharing open data to develop more than 100 digital mask maps. Chang is experienced in formulating design decisions for solving complex problems. Her aim is to shift the expectation that public services are 'supplied by the government to the people' to 'services that can be created by the people and the government together', thus forming an inclusive public service.

Based on Chang's design thinking for purchasing masks, an online mask reservation system was launched in a short period of time to allow people who don't have time to line up to purchase masks conveniently online. Chang says:

---

[47] Ibid.

[48] 'National Policy for Empowerment of Emirati Women - 2031'. *The United Arab Emirates' Government portal*. https://u.ae/en/about-the-uae/strategies-initiatives-and-awards/policies/social-affairs/national-policy-for-empowerment-of-emirati-women

[49] Yun Xuan Poon. 'Hao-Ting Chang, Design Lead, Public Digital Innovation Space, Taiwan'. *GovInsider*. December 2021. https://govinsider.asia/intl-en/article/hao-ting-chang-design-lead-public-digital-innovation-space-taiwan-women-in-govtech-2021

The "human-centered" thinking led us to re-examine the implementation, and a few weeks later, we launched the direct pre-order masks at convenience stores (with the help of shop assistants if needed). This was convenient for the elderly or others who are not familiar with technology or digital tools. After observing the needs of the people, we use various tools and technologies to assist us in designing policies.[50]

Karen Makishima, formerly Japan's Digital Minister is on a mission to provide 'human-friendly digitalization: No one left behind'.[51] Established in 2021, Makishima spearheaded Japan's Digital Agency which has taken proactive steps towards improving public IT infrastructure. It selected global IT firms to provide government cloud services, aiming to integrate fragmented local and central government IT services. During the pandemic, it quickly rolled out a nationwide database and app for confirming the vaccination status of the population. Makishima shares that during the pandemic the initial feedback was that Japan's digital efforts were slow, so when the new digital agency was set up, its aim was to be the control tower of a digital public sector and provide services directly to the public. Makishima explains:

We aim to create a "warm-hearted digital society" that is unique to Japan, where the benefits of digitalisation can be delivered while staying close to people who are not good at digital. In addition, to the digitalisation of government, we will also promote the digitalisation of society such as health, medical care, education, disaster risk management, and mobility.

---

[50] Ibid.

[51] Sean Nolan. 'Karen Makishima, Minister for Digital, Japan'. *GovInsider*. January 2022. https://govinsider.asia/intl-en/article/karen-makishima-ministerfor-digital-japan-women-in-govtech-2021

If we recognise current rules and laws are barriers to technology utilisation, we must reform them boldly.[52]

What are female digital economic agents?

We can understand the female digital revolution by understanding the different economic roles women play—as digital consumers, digital businesses, digital entrepreneurs and digital government. We observe how female consumer spending is boosting our economies and how small women-led businesses are servicing local communities. We also learn how women are leading digital transformational changes within large multinationals, tech companies, city councils, or government ministries. An analysis of the different roles guides us in tailoring strategies to train, employ, invest, and protect more women. We must also inspire the next generation of women and encourage women from all backgrounds to develop skills and transition into prosperous careers with high demand and higher pay.

---

[52] Sean Nolan. 'Karen Makishima, Minister for Digital, Japan'. *GovInsider*. January 2022. https://govinsider.asia/intl-en/article/karen-makishima-minister-for-digital-japan-women-in-govtech-2021/

Chapter 5

The Changemakers

'Most perceive their work as a fundamental aspect of their satisfaction in life and view their place of work as an integral part of their social world.'[1]

—Professor Claudia Goldin, Nobel Prize winner of Economic Sciences

What do you want to be when you grow up? We were always asked this question when we were at school. The reality is that at a young age, many children don't know what they want to do. As they explore their own interests, mission, and purpose in life the world changes too, driven by external forces like politics, international trade, climate change, changing demographics, and of course, technology. With the average person staying no longer that four years in one job, career paths are no longer linear, and many are making it their mission to change the world where there is economic, political, environmental, or social injustice. We call them changemakers. The concept of changemaking refers to anyone working to solve a problem by tackling the root cause rather than just treating the symptoms. Indeed, it can be 'anyone'.

---

[1] Claudia Goldin. 'The Quiet Revolution That Transformed Women's Employment, Education, and Family'. *AEA papers and proceedings*. May 2006. Vol. 96 No. 2.

Young girls from villages in developing countries, university students, female professionals in multinational companies, and female academics are becoming changemakers. For instance, Nobel Prize winner Professor Claudia Goldin has been recognized for advancing the understanding of women in the workplace in order to address the gender pay gap that continues to exist today. Her economic research finds that for women work is a 'vibrant facet of their identity and a profound source of personal and professional satisfaction'.[2] Described as a detective, she discovered that women over the decades had shifted from holding jobs to pursuing careers. In identifying what she described as a quiet revolution, she realized that the younger generation of women could forsee their future with options.

Women had expanded their horizons. 'Women more accurately anticipated their future work lives. With more accurate expectations, they could better prepare by investing in formal education and they could assume positions that involved advancement.'[3] According to Goldin, the revolutionary phase began with women born in the US in the late 1940s who became teenagers in the mid-1960s. 'These young women began to perceive that their adult lives would differ substantially from those of their mothers' generation. Their revised expectations of future employment, in turn, led young women to continue with college and to graduate.'[4]

In pursuit of a different future, Goldin's research showed that women shifted from traditional occupations like a teacher, nurse, or librarian to professional services like a lawyer, physician,

---

[2] Mara Marinakis. 'Claudia Goldin: Decoding the Evolution of Women in the Workforce'. *The W.O.M.A.N. Connection.* October 2023.

[3] Claudia Goldin. 'The Quiet Revolution That Transformed Women's Employment, Education, and Family'. *AEA papers and proceedings.* May 2006. Vol. 96 No. 2.

[4] Ibid.

or professor. In education, there was a shift too. Women moved away from studying traditional fields like literature, languages, and home economics and studied business. 'Women's majors shifted from those that were "consumption" related to those that were "investment" related.' By the 1970s, women in the US placed greater emphasis on recognition and career success.[5]

Career paths today are changing. Technological advancement like 3D Printing, algorithms, IoT, and cloud computing in our workplaces means that globally, 40 million to 160 million women may need to transition between occupations by 2030.[6] If they make these transitions, women could find more productive and better paid work. However, if women don't, they could face a growing wage gap if they lack digital skills, or they may end up leaving the workforce. Many women have already transitioned to working in the digital economy, particularly in jobs related to digital marketing or recruiting digital talent. These roles in HR and marketing have traditionally been undertaken by women. Other women have sought to work with technology in niche sectors or have chosen to break barriers in male-dominated industries. Whether it's to disrupt an industry, make use of the vast volumes of data being produced, create art, or put in place infrastructure or regulations to facilitate and protect the digital economy, women are playing a key role. Like Goldin, these women are changemakers. They can be found in our local towns, schools, or organizations and not just on the international stage. With high-speed internet access, they are using algorithms, data, blockchain, digital platforms, and mobile apps to drive with mission and purpose.

Next, we showcase real-life stories of inspiring women making impact in areas like agriculture, finance, creative arts, and health.

---

[5] Ibid.

[6] Anu Madgavkar, James Manyika, Mekala Krishnan, Kweilin Ellingrud, Lareina Yee, Jonathan Woetzel, Michael Chui, Vivian Hunt, and Sruti Balakrishnan. 'The future of women at work'. *McKinsey Global Institute*. June 2019.

These formidable changemakers want to solve urgent real-world problems like climate change, wars, poverty, and cybercrime. We take a look at what it's like to be a fintech startup, climate tech warrior, an AI doctor, datacentre designer, digital artist, cybersecurity specialist, data manager, and data privacy specialist. By sharing the career paths of other women, the hope is that women and teenage girls can see how they themselves can be part of the digital economy, in whatever way they want, as virtually every industry is being digitalized to some extent.

The Fintech Startup

> 'I was rejected for a credit card—even though I helped develop it. Now I'm on a mission to get all women the credit we deserve with Sequin.'[7]
>
> —Vrinda Gupta, CEO, Sequin Financial

Vrinda Gupta developed a credit card for women. She started developing the card for a large payment company but then was turned down for the product when she applied for it. She was disappointed as she had spent multiple years designing, launching, and scaling the credit card. The rejection spurred her to start her own company, Sequin Financial, which helps millions of women boost their credit ratings so that they can successfully obtain credit.

Women in the US have been allowed to apply for and own a credit card in their name since 1974, when the Equal Credit Opportunity Act was introduced. At that time, the women's rights movement became widespread, and women were gaining control over their own lives professionally and financially. However, today, women still have unequal access to credit. No credit card in their own name means no credit profile and no credit score. It's a vicious cycle. Based on her unfortunate experience, Gupta is leading a

---

[7] Vrinda Gupta website: https://www.vrinda-gupta.com/

movement to close the gender gap. Her company Sequin's mission is to make credit more approachable and engaging for women. If more women own a credit card, they can establish a credit history showing lenders that they are financially responsible for bigger purchases like car loans and mortgages. Gupta found that, 'All my years of smart budgeting and app payments didn't show up in my credit history. To big banks, I was invisible. If you've ever been rejected or hit your credit limit, you know the feeling.'[8]

Gupta was named one of New York City's 55 Most Inspiring Women in Fintech, and 92 per cent of Sequin's investors are female angels from consumer tech, financial services, and design industries. 'I'm inspired by women's progress and accomplishments, as inspirational leaders and innovators in an industry that was designed to leave women out of the narrative.'[9] More women leading and innovating like Gupta are needed in the fintech industry to cater to women. Around 45 million women have no bank account. Further, women account for 19 per cent of executives in fintech companies, 11 per cent of board members, and 1.5 per cent of founders.[10] Yet, many women are crying out for targeted support with managing their finances including spending, saving, borrowing, and financial planning. Especially as women's wealth increases, increasing their spending power. To address this need, Sequin has developed its own university. Developed by a group of female banking experts, Sequin built a credit curriculum which Gupta says is to make sure that 'all women get the banking (and financial knowledge!) we deserve'.[11]

---

[8] 'Episode #58: Credit Inequalities Against Women and How to Combat Them with Vrinda Gupta'. *Investor Mama Podcast.* March 2022.

[9] Joanna England. 'Top 10 women to watch in fintech for 2023.' *FinTech Magazine.* March 2023.

[10] The Fintech Diversity Radar 2021. https://findexable.com/diversity-radar/

[11] 'Introducing Sequin University'. *Sequin Blog.* November 2023. https://www.sequincard.com/blog/sequin-university/

The Climate Tech Activist

'We wanted to leverage science for the betterment of the planet, and we were inspired by this idea of, "remaking how things are made" through carbon transformation.'[12]

—Dr Lisa Dyson, co-founder, Air Protein

Dr Lisa Dyson is producing the world's first air-based meat. By combining air, water, and mineral nutrients, this protein source has the potential to feed the growing population and mitigate climate change, if adopted on a global scale.

We started exploring how we could make food production more sustainable. It's an area where we can make some of the greatest strides in slowing climate change and also align with the rising demand from consumers and industry for more sustainable food. From there, Air Protein was born.[13]

Dr Dyson, a scientist and entrepreneur, witnessed the devastation caused by weather-related disasters and has since been on a mission to address climate change, in particular food security. Land used for cattle and animal feed production is leading to deforestation. Cattle itself is one of the major contributors of greenhouse gas emissions. The challenges with food security and climate change received attention in 2023's United Nations Climate Change Conference, more commonly known as COP28. Around 140 nations signed a declaration to include food and agriculture in their prevention of climate change plans, and more than 130 recognized the need to shift to sustainable healthy diets.

---

[12] John Greathouse. 'Here's How Lisa Dyson's Startup Is Reducing World Hunger AND Combating Climate Change.' *Forbes*. March 2020.

[13] Theodora Aidoo. 'Lisa Dyson: the woman creating the world's first air-based meat'. *Face2face Africa*. April 2020.

Air-based meat offers a solution that allows farmers to increase food production by 70 per cent, with only a 5 per cent land increase to feed a global population of 10 billion people by 2050.[14] Dr Dyson describes the process of making air meat like making yoghurt:

> First, we start with elements from the air we breathe, carbon dioxide, oxygen and nitrogen and combine these elements with water and mineral nutrients. Next, we use renewable energy and a probiotic production process where cultures convert the elements into nutrients.[15]

She discovered the technological process from a space programme. In the 1970s, NASA scientists explored a way to feed astronauts on long space journeys. Astronauts used microbes called hydrogenotrophs to convert carbon dioxide in exhaled breath into nutrient-rich crops. Dr Dyson started to grow microbes in her lab, working with manufacturers to scale-up their technology to develop sustainable food production.

The technology to produce the protein can be made in days instead of months regardless of weather conditions. It also requires significantly less water and land, allowing farms to expand vertically with geographic flexibility. The Air Protein website explains that, 'Making food doesn't have to mean deforestation, industrial animal farming, or reliance on systems that emit massive amounts of greenhouse gases that harm our planet.'[16]

Food security is only one aspect of addressing climate change as other climate technologies are being developed, like

---

[14] 'Global Agricultural towards 2050.' United Nations Food and Agricultural Foundation. October 2009.

[15] John Greathouse. 'Here's How Lisa Dyson's Startup Is Reducing World Hunger AND Combating Climate Change'. *Forbes*. March 2020.

[16] Air Protein website: https://www.airprotein.com/

technologies used to reduce carbon, develop renewal energy (such as wind, solar, and hydropower) and zero emission transport. You may recall at the start of this journey, when learning about the female digital economy, we found that women tend to have greater care for the planet.[17] Here we learn how Dr Dyson is leveraging the power of climate technology to enable positive environmental and societal change.[18] Dr Dyson is the fourth African American woman in history to earn a PhD in theoretical physics and was inspired by her father to follow an entrepreneurial path. 'My dad was an entrepreneur . . . he ultimately was the president of a chain of 55 hair salons, so entrepreneurship is kind of in my blood.'[19]

By empowering women and girls globally, a study calculated that we could avoid 120 billion tons of emissions by 2050, which is approximately ten years' worth of China's annual emissions as of 2014. There is an influx of female scientists and technologists, building and scaling companies with climate and sustainable industry implications. Dr Dyson's mission to solve global hunger and the planet is just one example.

The AI Doctor

'I'd always been really creative at school. I loved doing art projects and technology projects and building things. I missed those aspects when practicing medicine.'[20]

—Dr Claire Novorol, chief medical officer, Ada

---

[17] Elle Hunt. 'The eco gender gap: why is saving the planet seen as women's work?' *The Guardian*. February 2020.

[18] 'Greening Household Behavior: Overview from the 2011 Survey-Revised edition'. *OECD Studies on Environmental Policy and Household Behaviour*.

[19] John Greathouse. 'Here's How Lisa Dyson's Startup Is Reducing World Hunger AND Combating Climate Change'. *Forbes*. March 2020.

[20] Ashley Osiason. 'Interview with Co-Founder and Chief Medical Officer of Ada Health, Dr. Claire Novorol'. *Wharton Undergraduate Founders and Funders*. June 2021.

Dr Claire Novorol teaches people to understand their health and figure out what to do when something might be wrong.[21] Inspired to find a creative solution to real-life problems, she developed an AI-based app that allows users to track their symptoms and navigate next steps with health professionals. Her health app is called Ada, named after the first computer programmer, Ada Lovelace, as discussed in Chapter two. The Ada Health app has been downloaded by 4 million users and has been used to complete over 6 million health assessments.[22] It has been ranked as the top medical app in over 130 countries.

Dr Novorol created an app so people could understand their symptoms with a free symptom checker, built on AI and clinical evidence. The Ada Health app provides care options based on your symptoms and health profile. Growing up, Dr Novorol says that she was interested in many different things but chose science:

> I was pretty good at sciences, and there was a really good sciences department at my school, so I ended up choosing those subjects. I thought medicine could be really interesting because I could apply science but also work with people and feel like I'm doing something to make an impact.[23]

However, starting a company was never on her career agenda. 'I did not always know that I wanted to start a company. Even once I was a doctor, I found myself searching for the right fit for me. I started as a hospital doctor, I tried adult medicine, I moved

---

[21] 'Claire Novorol: Entrepreneurship Expert'. *Said Business School. University of Oxford.* https://www.sbs.ox.ac.uk/about-us/people/claire-novorol

[22] 'Claire Novorol'. *Forbes Profile.* https://www.forbes.com/profile/claire-novorol/?sh=5408fb4b2e64

[23] Ashley Osiason. 'Interview with Co-Founder and Chief Medical Officer of Ada Health, Dr. Claire Novorol'. *Wharton Undergraduate Founders and Funders.* June 2021.

into paediatrics in hospitals, and then I moved into genetics.'[24] While studying for her PhD at Cambridge, Dr Novorol met several people at the business school as the college encouraged cross-disciplinary socializing and discussions. 'I started going along to some entrepreneurship speaker events, and I found them really fascinating and inspiring.'[25]

At Ada, Dr Novorol is responsible for overseeing medical affairs, clinical partnerships, and for ensuring that Ada's products are tailored to support patient needs. On her journey, she has advised several health start-ups and also founded Doctorpreneurs, a global community of over 6000 medical professionals interested in health entrepreneurship.[26] While working with a lot of data and AI based tools, she points out the importance of keeping with technology and relevant regulation:

> It's a fast-changing space. Since we first launched, a lot has changed in terms of what requires regulation: whether or not something is considered a medical device, the regulation of software as a medical device, evolving thoughts on AI within medicine, and of course, GDPR (General Data Protection Regulation).[27]

The Ada health app is free to customers but makes its money from partnerships with companies in the health system, including insurers and life science businesses. The majority of those partnerships are in the US and Europe, with some partnerships in Africa. Dr Novorol's story shows how AI can be used to make

---

[24] Ibid.

[25] Ibid.

[26] 'Opportunities Board for Doctors now LIVE!' Doctorpreneurs website.

[27] Ibid.

a difference and that you don't need to start with a qualification in computing.

The Datacentre Designer

'It's a fascinating career to have, you never get bored. If you're a learner, it's a fun industry to be in. it just makes me sad that it's so non-inclusive.'[28]

—Nancy Novak, chief innovation officer,
Compass Datacenters

Nancy Novak followed in her father's footsteps and spent her career in the construction industry. She studied construction engineering and with over twenty-five years of construction experience, she oversaw the delivery of over $3.5 billion in projects. Some of those projects included building data centres—the power houses of the AI and data revolution. It is the physical facility that stores any company's digital data. A data centre is a building that stores computing machines and related hardware such as servers, data storage drives, and network equipment. After a period of retirement, Novak returned to work inspired to build the growing number of data centres around the world. 'The CEO of Compass Datacenters asked me to come and help him build Compass. This was a fantastic opportunity for me,' says Novak. 'I consider myself a true builder. I've done everything from launch pads, to airports, to hospitals and museums . . . And then data centers.'[29]

If you've ever visited a data centre, it can often look like you're in a sci-fi movie. There are rows of servers, cooling towers, and lots

---

[28] Eloise Brown. 'In Conversation With: Nancy Novak, Compass Datacenters'. *Data Center People Blog*. March 2021. https://www.datacenterpeople.com/blog/in-conversation-with-nancy-novak-compass-datacenters

[29] Ibid.

of network cables. Data centres allow businesses to adopt cloud computing. This includes data-driven businesses like e-commerce companies, logistics providers, banks, and insurance companies, as well as hospitals, schools, and universities—all of which need significant data management, storage, recovery, and backup support for large volumes of online transactions and applications like e-mails and payment gateways. The different types of data centres in cloud computing are infrastructure-as-a-service (IaaS), software-as-a-service (SaaS), and platform-as-a-service (PaaS). Novak wants to make the construction of data centres better.

> Honestly, the thing that attracted me to Compass was their desire to disrupt the industry. We have figured out how to make some repeatable facilities, where we can learn and get better. There is so much construction with data centrers on a global scale, and there's so much to do! These big tech firms that Compass services are somewhat new in the construction industry.[30]

As Novak highlights, the demand for data centres is growing. The construction industry as a whole is growing at around 4 per cent per year and data centre construction is growing at 8 per cent. The US has the highest number of cloud data centres, followed by Germany, the UK, and then India. In line with this demand is a greater need for people to work in data centres, which is also attracting high salaries. The number of staff needed to run data centres will grow from around two million to nearly 2.3 million by 2025. Popular positions include data centre technicians, facility engineers, electricians, production leaders, engineers, project managers, and maintenance technicians.

However, the proportion of women working in data centres remains low. More than three-quarters of data centre operators surveyed, report that their workforce is around 10 per cent women

---

[30] Ibid.

or less. What's more, almost one in four companies have no women as part of their design, build, and operations staff. Novak has been active in trying to make the industry more inclusive. She is involved in a number of organizations dedicated to the advancement of woman in business. She has even participated in the White House Women and Diversity STEM forums. Novak devotes her spare time to helping other women.

> I'll have lunch, coffee or get on a call with people; especially young women. I want to mentor young women. The biggest advantage that men have in our industry, is the potential vs. credential conundrum. We, as women, could have every credential, but we don't have the relationships that can be built in an organic setting that allows leadership to see our potential.[31]

Her advice to women thinking about a career working in data centres is to network, network, and network. She also shares, 'there are tonnes of industries that have wonderful transferable skills and attributes that our industry needs, so having no experience in the data centre industry is no dealbreaker.'[32] With attractive salaries, the industry has opportunities for women. An American survey showed that half of all data centre professionals reported annual salaries of $100,000 or greater, with nearly 10 per cent reporting salaries at or above $200,000.

The Digital Artist

> 'I want younger viewers to see themselves within my work, as I couldn't see myself in books, media and films growing up.'[33]
>
> —Nourie Flayhan, illustrator

---

[31] Ibid.

[32] Ibid.

[33] Chekii Harling. 'Daydreaming with Nourie Flayhan'. *Selfridges*. https://www.selfridges.com/SG/en/features/articles/selfridges-meets/nourie-flayhan/

Nourie Flayhan introduces herself as a storyteller and illustrator from the mountains of Lebanon. Her art has been described as warming and full of childhood memories—all of which are produced as digital art. There are no paintbrushes, and the canvas is a computer screen. Digital art is anything produced or made on digital media, such as animations, photographs, illustrations, videos, and digital paintings. Artists must have creative skills but must also be proficient with working with different software on a computer or tablet. Growing up, Flayhan enjoyed drawing and traded ink and pen for a tablet.

> My brother is an architect and I remember him saying, "Why don't you digitise your illustrations? You can use a tablet or scan in your drawings to manipulate them." With ink, I would have to start from scratch if I messed up but using a Wacom tablet meant I could edit my work as I went along. Two years ago, I switched to using an iPad.[34]

Flayhan, born to Lebanese immigrants fleeing war, was raised in Kuwait and attended art school in the UK. She was most comfortable expressing herself through her art in the security and comfort of her home with her brothers and parents and it was only at university that she found her own voice. Now based in Dubai, she feels she has a responsibility. 'I am a diaspora child, so I always had a connection to home but never felt like I belonged anywhere. I would hear stories about how women were treated in my home country and felt I had a social responsibility to share the knowledge I had come across.'[35]

Digital art has countless applications but is most commonly used in commercial settings. These include media advertisements,

---

[34] Ibid.

[35] Ibid.

films, and video games that need visual graphic effects and animations. Flayhan's digital art is internationally recognized, and she has collaborated with big brands like Gucci Beauty, House of Aama, Carolina Herrera, and Vogue. 'Gucci was a dream for me because I feel so connected to Alessandro Michele's magical vision. More recently, I've been using my platform to highlight designers from within our region who are starting out with sustainable brands.'[36]

Most recently, she collaborated with Adidas for a limited edition collection of T-shirts and hoodies celebrating Ramadan. Her art included the UAE's emblems—the palm tree, henna, and seven stars to honour the seven Emirates—interpreted through Flayhan's illustration style. Flayhan has even worked with the mobile phone maker Samsung. In an advertising campaign for the Galaxy Z Flip5, Flayhan tells her story of her artwork. The campaign follows Flayhan as she searches for new sources of inspiration and reflects on the places where culture is cultivated.[37]

Digital art is accessible, global, and widely influential. Artists can conveniently store and deliver their art making several prints. Thus, the ease of publishing, sharing, and selling digital art has made many new jobs and careers available for digital artists all around the world. The online global art market is predicted to increase by 494 per cent in 2024. The growth of online communities and marketplaces has created a thriving ecosystem for digital artists, providing them with a platform to showcase their works and connect with audiences around the world.[38] As the use

---

[36] Ibid.

[37] 'Samsung Unfolds a Story of Artistic Inspiration with Illustrator Nourie Flayhan'. *Hypebeast*. September 2023. https://hypebeast.com/2023/9/samsung-nourie-flayhan-limited-edition-collection-campaign

[38] Charlotte Stewart. 'The Online Global Art Market Around The World'. *My Art Broker*

of technology in the art landscape evolves, especially in relation to AR and VAR (discussed in Chapter two), there are opportunities for women to showcase their talent and have diverse voices and feelings expressed through art.

The Cybersecurity Specialist

'Recruiters are looking for women to work in cybersecurity-its like looking for exotic species!'[39]

—Shiguftah Malik, principal information security consultant, Gemserv

'Good morning, everyone, welcome to cybersecurity training.' Shiguftah works in the cyber and privacy department of a company. As a highly experienced consultant with in-depth knowledge of cybersecurity, she was anxious. The night before she was scheduled to deliver cybersecurity training, she struggled to sleep. She had stayed up late to prepare. She kept thinking of all the possible questions that the course participants might ask. She wanted to make sure she had all the answers, especially as her audience were always men. Many of these men looked at her in surprise or struggled to take her seriously as a cybersecurity specialist. Yet, Malik was an accomplished security expert. Having gained certifications, she specialized in implementing and auditing information security and data protection management systems in different sectors. When training, the male students would stare at Malik, alarmed that a woman was going to train them. After all, what could she possibly teach them? At least, that is what Malik thought.

But Malik was on a mission. She wanted to nudge people's behaviour in understanding the serious threat of cyberattacks when working online. She was aware that there had been a number

---

[39] Nimisha Tailor. Interview with Shiguftah Malik. November 2023.

of significant and costly data breaches by large British companies. For example, the £20 million fine imposed on the airline carrier, British Airway (BA), for a data breach had put cybersecurity in the spotlight.[40] The incident took place when BA's systems were compromised by attackers. Data was stolen including payment and travel booking details as well as name and addresses of travellers. A government investigation concluded that the airline had not put in place sufficient security measures at that time. This is where a cybersecurity specialist can help. Their job entails providing protection during software development. They work to make sure that networks are safe from external threats like hackers, who want access for malicious purposes. To effectively protect an organization's network and infrastructure, most cybersecurity professionals must learn how to 'ethically hack'. Essentially, you need to have the same skills as a hacker to fully understand how a system could be breached, and in turn, create effective solutions for thwarting these attacks.

On the day of the training, Malik's day had started well, and she was pleased with how the course was going. But as the day progressed, she got more and more agitated. During the training, an operations director started asking a number of questions. He asked one question, then another. He just wouldn't stop. The rest of the course participants stayed silent and watched the male director and Malik have a ping-pong match of question and answer. After the session, Malik was relieved that the session had ended and she could now relax. To her disbelief, the male director approached her. In a quiet voice he said, 'No one has ever been able to answer all my questions.'

Cybersecurity is one of the fast-growing fields in a variety of sectors with problem-solving a major feature of day-to-day work. Malik has assisted many companies manage their information

---

[40] Joe Tidy. 'British Airways fined £20m over data breach'. *BBC*. October 2020. https://www.bbc.com/news/technology-54568784

security and data protection risks, by ensuring the client's policies and procedures are compliant with industry best practices and regulations. She has become used to walking into a room full of men. Her advice to women is 'to show your talents and always find ways to expand your knowledge and experience. Set your sights high and then aim higher than that. You should always believe in yourself'. She commented:

> Everyone brings their own uniqueness to the role irrespective of their gender. Women have many talents, however, this is often overlooked as women are perceived to be emotional or aggressive where in fact they are being firm. Women should be allowed to be . . . firm and assertive and hold their ground without any negative connotations.[41]

The global cybersecurity workforce was short of some 3.5 million workers in 2021, highlighting a clear opportunity for women to use their problem-solving skills and grow the cybersecurity workforce. Malik shares that as a consultant she has come across many companies where IT departments are still very much male dominated. Her solution is that having more women representatives at tech talks and career fairs would change the status quo.[42]

The Data Manager

> 'Data is all around us and we continue to interact with it on a daily basis.'[43]
>
> —Tamzyn Bielecka, former data manager,
> British Petroleum

[41] 'IWD 2023 | Shiguftah Malik, Senior Information Security Consultant'. *Gemserv*. https://www.youtube.com/watch?v=GfadWnz7t2g

[42] 'Women in Tech: What The Experts Say . . .'. *TechRound*. March 2021.

[43] Yellowfin Team. 'She Loves Discovering Data'. *Yellowfin Blog*.

It was the nineteenth time that year that Tamzyn Bielecka was being asked to travel outside of London to help a client. She had got used to travelling, but not through choice. She had been with the company for two years and wasn't sure why she was being sent out of the office all the time. Did her boss not like her, or was it her colleagues? Did they find her disruptive? These are the thoughts that went through Bielecka's mind, as she sat in her boss' office who was explaining that she urgently needed to get herself to Manchester. Bielecka was passionate about technology and studied IT and robotics in Canberra, Australia. Working in London as her first job, she was a long way away from home, but the consulting firm she worked for was a great opportunity. Before she could respond to the request to travel, Bielecka suddenly found herself sobbing. Overwhelmed with frustration and confusion, and wiping tears from her eyes, she upsettingly asked, 'Why me? Why are you sending me away again?' Her boss looked at her, astonished. 'You are the person I trust! You get things done. I can send you to the client and I know their problem will be fixed.' As her boss talked, in a matter-of-fact tone, Bielecka sunk into her chair and a penny dropped inside her head. She was good at her job. She had been doubting herself.

Years later, Bielecka led a data team for a global energy company and worked as a data manager. In this role, she delivered multiple major projects using global data sets. As we become more digitalized, the amount of data produced is expected to increase.[44] We are also producing large volumes of different types of data. When we WhatsApp or comment on social media, we generate personal data. When we buy lunch or shop online, we generate financial data when we pay. When we go to the doctor, have scans and blood tests, we generate health data. When we catch the bus or

---

[44] Bernard Marr & Co. *Statista*. https://explodingtopics.com/blog/data-generated-per-day

train, we generate transport data when we tap our transport card on the automated machines. With all this data there are so many insights to be gleaned that can help organizations be faster, leaner, and serve customers more efficiently.

Bielecka knows how to guide companies to make better use of their data. 'I am bloody good at data. I know how to use it and how to make it work.'[45] Data science involves gaining useful insights from large amounts of unstructured data using software, data mining, and statistical methods, algorithms, and machine learning principles. Data scientists figure out what the data means, look for patterns, and find openings so they can inform businesses' decision-making. Working in this profession, Bielecka is recognized as an industry expert for large-scale, complex, and modern data platforms with experience across all things data like data integration, data migration, data analytics, and data warehousing. She has a strong business acumen in customer loyalty, campaigns, retail and distribution of goods. Bielecka's skillset is in high demand. In the US, data scientist jobs are predicted to rise by 36 per cent between 2021 and 2031.

Globally, companies are struggling to make sense of the vast amounts of data at their disposal and figuring out how to handle large datasets. Banks, insurance companies, retail businesses, healthcare providers, and government agencies are all in need of data scientists. However, in 2020, only 15 per cent[46] of data scientists in the UK were women. Yet, data science will grow more than any other field by 2029.[47] Bielecka has been an inspiration for other women, and mentors in her free time encouraging young women to pursue, or women thinking of switching to, a career involving data. Through mentoring, she helps women realize that

---

[45] Nimisha Tailor. Interview with Tamzyn Bielecka. October 2023.

[46] 'Girls in data: Inspiring the future of female data science'. *Open Access Government*. December 2022.

[47] 'Data Science insights: job and market growth stats'. *Future Learn*. March 2021.

data is everywhere, and it is not something to be feared. It can be as simple as numbers on a spreadsheet, or can be as complex as using a data model. Bielecka has taught courses organized by She Loves Data, a social enterprise that organizes events and workshops to make women more data-literate.[48]

> You don't have to be the smartest person in the room. I wish someone had told me that earlier in my career. At high school and university, I spent a lot of energy on competing with the crowd and being hard on myself because of challenges with dyslexia. But it didn't take me too long to realise and play to my strengths of data and coding in SQL. I found that with these skills as my foundations, I can work through any changes faced in this scary fast technology changing world. Foundations are FUNdamental![49]

Data Privacy Professional

> 'GDPR has significantly increased public awareness of the importance of data protection, which in turn has raised the profile of privacy and data protection on the corporate agenda.'[50]
> —Natasha Warner, former head of privacy and information management, Direct Line Group

The digital economy is being powered by copious amounts of data. But some of that data is private. It's personal and confidential. So, companies that collect personal data like credit card details,

---

[48] She Loves Data website: https://www.shelovesdata.com/about-us/

[49] Pavel. 'How to break into the tech industry and create a rewarding career'. *She Loves Data*. September 2019. https://www.shelovesdata.com/2019/09/24/how-to-break-into-the-tech-industry-and-create-a-rewarding-career/

[50] Philippa Donn. 'GDPR 5 years on'. *Data Protection Network*. May 2023. https://dpnetwork.org.uk/gdpr-5-years-on/

passport details, or store and manage business data like sales, must take adequate steps to protect it. But whose job is it? Natasha Warner used to work for a large insurance company where vast amounts of claims are processed every day containing personal details of individuals and companies. Within the company, Warner led a team of privacy and information management professionals 'advising on all things data protection' to ensure that the insurance company is 'doing the right thing by customers' and employees' personal data'.[51] The UK company sold a wide range of insurance products, including car insurance, home insurance, and travel insurance. Warner's team worked closely with the company's security team to ensure 'the data is kept secure, as well as ensuring all personal and corporate information is handled in line with company policy'.

In light of the growing concerns about privacy, governments around the world have been introducing policies and regulations on data protection and privacy. Data privacy defines who has access to data, while data protection provides tools and policies to actually restrict/protect access to the data. It is estimated that out of 194 countries, 66 per cent have legislation in place for securing the protection of data and privacy and 10 per cent have draft legislation. The data privacy regulatory environment is evolving, and companies are increasingly looking for professionals to understand and comply with new laws. Ever since the data protection law, GDPR came in to force in the European Union in 2018, there has been a wave of similar digital privacy legislation. The rising trend for remote work and cloud-based services spurred by the Covid-19 pandemic has also increased the demand for privacy experts to address the wave of data privacy issues.

---

[51] 'Direct line group – Natasha Warner, Head of Privacy and Information'. *Women in tech.*

Warner transitioned to her job with guidance from a mentor. She says:

> I grew into my career after I moved from teaching in 2005 and took a position as records assistant at a large international manufacturer. Whilst there, I was mentored by a senior female leader and I became Privacy Manager, building controls and processes from the ground up.[52]

Data privacy roles involves using encryption to manage and store sensitive information, determining when or if to share information with others, and creating company policies to ensure employees do not inadvertently violate privacy protection laws. Warner invested in herself and completed a Master's in Information Rights Law and began an apprenticeship degree in Data Science. She progressed quickly within the insurance company and became part of the Information Security, Risk and Assurance Leadership Team. Warner's role required a combination of technical and soft skills, such as expert knowledge of data protection laws, technical and analytical skills, communication skills, and ethical and professional qualities.[53] She is known to be always willing to challenge the norm in a pragmatic and risk weighted way, and is now managing privacy for a global credit card company. To encourage more women into the technology sector, Warner thinks that there is a need to ensure 'that women understand the range of roles available in the technology space, and the different ways in which they contribute to business, as well as (as is the case for privacy roles) the benefits for society, will

---

[52] Ibid.

[53] Ibid.

help to entice women to study technology related courses'.[54] Her view is that there 'shouldn't be barriers for women getting into tech, but society's perceptions on what technology roles are like and the stereotypes associated with people who go into technology roles may be hindering women from entering these professions'. Her solution is to showcase 'more technology roles available, evidencing a range of diverse women who are working in these roles and inviting more young people to explore these roles through placements and internships'.[55]

Who are the Changemakers?

There are so many different careers that women can pursue in the digital economy. Some are technical, like software engineering, cloud computing, designing data centres, while others require digital leadership skills. Women can choose the path that suits and interests them and be inspired by the women that have already digitally transformed their careers. With a greater understanding of the careers available, the next step is to understand how can women transition to these jobs? How can young girls get future ready and learn key skills and knowledge? Let us discover this in the next chapter.

---

[54] Ibid.

[55] Ibid.

Chapter 6

Digital Skills

'Learning will become a lifelong process, the biggest activity on the planet and the major growth market of the twenty-first century.'[1]

—Dr Alan Burton-Jones, Griffith University

The four industrial revolutions have changed the products and services we consume, the types of businesses providing them, and the jobs available to produce them. The nature of work tasks and the skills needed have gone through a significant transformation. Since 1960, with the shift away from factory jobs, people spend considerably more of their working hours doing non-routine tasks that require higher order, analytical thinking, and interpersonal skills.[2] As more businesses adopt AI tools, this trend is expected to continue. Automation and AI are increasing productivity by carrying out repetitive, routine tasks and thinking systematically. It is estimated that 40 per cent of the average workday could be automated. Freeing up half a day would give workers more time on complex tasks and strategic activities.

---

[1] Alan Burton-Jones. *Knowledge Capitalism*. Oxford University Press. 1999.

[2] 'Future of Education and Skills 2030 project background'. *OECD*. 2019.

As a result, schools and universities are adapting to train the future workforce for a new technological environment. So far, school curriculum has shifted from a 'static, linear learning-progression model' to a 'non-linear, dynamic model', which recognizes that each student has their own learning path and is equipped with different prior knowledge, skills, and attitudes when they start school.[3]

As the future of work evolves, increasing the representation of women in the workforce from the current 50 per cent global rate highlighted in Chapter three is vital, women must ensure that they are skilled in applying creativity and critical thinking skills and engaging in constant learning to stay ahead of the game. Upskilling is needed for the short term, for instance, for women re-entering the workforce or switching careers. In the long-term, skill development is essential for young girls. The great news is that in general, women tend to possess the very core skills the digital economy requires. Women are good at communicating, problem-solving, and finding solutions by thinking outside of the box. If you are a Marvel fan, you will know Shuri, the Black Panther in the kingdom Wakanda. Shuri is naturally intelligent and a diplomatic leader. But she is also a phenomenal engineer with a strong understanding of Wakandan technology.[4] In many ways, women are like Shuri. In technical jobs like writing software code, women have performed well, staying calm and patient when adapting to constant changes and challenges. In leadership roles, women are known to be strong collaborators, which is essential as technology cuts across all sectors and disciplines.

Women and girls can be inspired to take on future digital jobs by pursuing not just ad hoc training but 'lifelong learning',

---

[3] Ibid.

[4] 'Shuri (Earth-616)'. *Marvel Database. Fandom Wiki.* https://marvel.fandom.com/wiki/Shuri_(Earth-616)

which is just as beneficial to men. Nok Anulomsombut, a CEO from a large technology company in Thailand, says that you can 'always learn about tech itself on the job. It's a lifelong learning, and we need to keep adapting to new technology that will come'.[5] The OECD reported that 'lifelong learning' will not only benefit individuals personally but the economy too. 'A skilled workforce makes it easier for firms to develop and introduce new technologies and work organization practices, thereby boosting productivity and growth in the economy as a whole.'[6] Karie Willyerd and Barbara Mistick, leaders in personal development and learning, recommend lifelong learning to stay relevant in the workforce.[7] With Willyerd's experience of leading multinational companies, and Mistick's leadership in the American education sector, the experts recommend: learning on the fly in any situation; opening your thinking to a world beyond where you are now; connect with people who can help you make your future happen; and stay motivated through the ups and downs of a career.

To learn more about digital skills, we show the importance of developing technical skills, especially for jobs like software engineering and cloud computing, but also the importance of digital leadership and entrepreneurship. We draw on examples from India, Southeast Asia, and New Zealand to share how these countries and regions are training young girls and women to code, understand cloud computing, tinker, and develop strong leadership skills.

---

[5] Vaishali Rastogi, Michael Meyer, Michael Tan, and Justine Tasiaux. 'Boosting Women in Technology in Southeast Asia'. October 2020.

[6] 'Support business dynamism and inclusive labour markets', in *Opportunities for All: A Framework for Policy Action on Inclusive Growth*. OECD Publishing, Paris. 2018. https://doi.org/10.1787/9789264301665-6-en.

[7] Karie Willyerd and Barbara Mistick. *Stretch: How to Future-Proof Yourself for Tomorrow's Workplace*. Wiley. 2016.

Learning to Code

'In the coming decade, there will be a good strength of
female professionals in the coding sector, as the schools have
introduced coding and girls are picking up well.'[8]

—Rajeev Tiwari, co-founder, Stemrobo Technologies

Thaslima Ferdous left the UK public health service to become
a data engineer. 'The NHS was really struggling and I felt
unappreciated,'[9] she says. After reading a story about a young
woman who had become a coder, she began to wonder if
she could switch careers, but was sceptical as she had a pure
science background. Ferdous studied biomedical science at
university. She wanted to become a doctor, so was working
as a healthcare assistant in London. Nonetheless, she gave
coding a try. 'I began to think "what do I have to lose?" So
decided to do a 14-week coding bootcamp which taught me
the foundations of python and SQL. My team is entirely male
but this is the start.'[10]

Today, many women are learning to code to improve job
prospects, and in some cases, like Ferdous, switch to more
fulfilling careers. Coding is essentially a conversation between a
computer operating system and the developer. Communication
is a key skill. Women have a reputation for communicating
more eloquently than men and are being drawn to coding.
And they are doing well. Although men make up 91 per cent
of the US software development industry, researchers in a
gender-blind study discovered that code written by women

---

[8] Puniti Pandey. 'Why the future belongs to female coders'. *The Times of India.*
March 2022.

[9] Shiona McCallum. 'The women who left their jobs to code'. *BBC.* April 2023.
https://www.bbc.com/news/technology-65175900

[10] Ibid.

was approved at a higher rate (78.6 per cent) than software code written by men (74.6 per cent).[11] In fact, as we learned in Chapter two, the world's first computer programmer in 1840 was Ada Lovelace.

Out of more than 1,200 women surveyed across the UK, women were switching to a career involving technology after working in professions like teaching, accountancy, retail, and healthcare.[12] In 2021, the number of women in the UK working as programmers and software developers increased by almost 15,000 on the year before, and the number of women working as web designers increased by almost 10,000. At the same time, more than 152,500 women left teaching, and 100,000 women left the nursing profession.

With more companies digitalizing, employers are increasingly looking for evidence of technical and interpersonal skills. Adding a programming language can help. If you work in a people-focused role, learning to code can strengthen your reasoning and logic skills. If you work in an analytical role, coding can sharpen your ability to work with data. Coding projects also develop creativity skills. Steve Jobs, the co-founder of Apple, once said, 'Everybody should learn to program a computer, because it teaches you how to think.' Coding trains your brain to think deeply, identify the problem, break things up, and then put the pieces together with a solution.

There are many free programmes teaching girls and women to code. Female-founded, Code First Girls[13] has delivered over £75 million worth of free coding courses to 150,000 women

---

[11] Sara Ashley O'Brien. 'Women coders do better than men in gender-blind study'. *CNN Business*. February 2016.

[12] Anugraha Sundaravelu. 'More women are quitting their jobs as teachers and nurses to become computer coders'. *Metro*. April 2023.

[13] Operates in the UK, Ireland, the US, Switzerland, and the Netherlands.

in the UK. The free education has boosted the women's employability as companies are connected to the newly trained female developers for potential jobs. Anna Brailsford, chief executive of the social enterprise, says women need to think differently about careers in STEM. 'There is a whole pool of untapped talent amongst those who started out in different fields of study and in different careers.'[14] In the US, there are at least thirty-three organizations that teach coding for women and girls. They include intensive coding bootcamps, coding classes, and coding scholarships for women.[15]

Women trained in coding have been able to apply these skills and develop promising careers in start-ups, government agencies, and large technology companies. For example, Ruchi Sanghvi was the first female engineer hired by Facebook. Sanghvi grew up in Pune, India, and was one of the main people writing code for the first version of Facebook's News Feed product. India's education and technology industry has been found to be more conducive to gender equality in computer programming. As a result, India has the largest proportion of female software developers, with a share of 23 per cent, while China ranks fourth at 20 per cent.[16] Rajeev Tiwari, co-founder of Stemrobo Technologies, provides STEM education programmes to schools in India. Their curriculum covers a wide range of subjects, including robotics, AI, and IoT, enabling students to gain hands-on experience and develop

---

[14] Shiona McCallum. 'The women who left their jobs to code'. BBC. April 2023. https://www.bbc.com/news/technology-65175900

[15] '33 Coding Programs for Women & Girls (Plus 9 Scholarships)'. *Learn to Code.* https://learntocodewith.me/posts/13-places-women-learn-code/

[16] Ritika Trikha. 'Which Countries Have the Most Female Developers?' *Hacker Rank.* January 2017. https://www.hackerrank.com/blog/which-countries-have-the-most-skilled-female-developers/

critical skills. Tiwari says that in schools, more girls are taking classes in coding and AI, compared to the past.[17]

Cloud Computing Certification

'Many women don't see themselves as qualified or a 'fit' for the cloud industry, but the things they think are holding them back might just be the skills that help them rise.'[18]
—Erica Schultz, president of field operations, Confluent

Veliswa Boya is one of South Africa's first black female cloud engineers. When cloud computing started being adopted by businesses in South Africa, she was excited.

I have always loved all things technology. When I first came to know about the cloud, I was really excited by how it is so central to innovation. This ultimately influences how businesses are able to offer faster time-to-market for products, better customer service, and better products to their customers.[19]

The cloud is a fancy way of describing a place where you can store and access things like pictures, documents, and videos over the internet instead of keeping them on your own computer or phone. That way, you can use any device with an internet connection to access your files from anywhere. For businesses, with large volumes of files, the cloud provides storage by using remote

---

[17] Puniti Pandey. 'Why the future belongs to female coders'. *The Times of India.* March 2022.

[18] Gabby Shacknai. 'The female founders hoping to fix gender disparity in cloud tech'. *Fortune.* October 2022.

[19] Evan-Lee Courie. 'Meet Veliswa Boya, one of SA's first black female cloud engineers'. *Biz Community South Africa.* September 2019. https://www.bizcommunity.com/Article/196/664/195149.html#

servers to store, access, and maintain data, instead of relying on local hard drives. Boya explains:

> If you use Netflix or use Airbnb from time to time, you are consuming products of a business that is using the cloud. Cloud is the consumption of remote resources or services, via the internet, provided to you by a third-party service provider. The consumption of cloud services is offered on a pay-as-you-go basis, which saves you upfront costs that you would normally incur when buying your own equipment to host these services inside your premises.[20]

The cloud industry in South Africa is one of the most developed in sub-Saharan Africa. In fact, cloud computing is growing around the world and is estimated to reach $1555 billion by 2030.[21]

Boya was familiar with Amazon Web Services (AWS), a global cloud computing company, and started learning by reading up on the company's services, watching lots of webinars, and building things using the services available. AWS offers different cloud computing products and services which includes servers, storage, networking, remote computing, email, mobile development, and security. After a period of self-learning, Boya decided to validate what she felt she knew by studying towards the certifications on offer. She then gained the opportunity to work at Standard Bank which had partnered with AWS. She joined the cloud team as one of the cloud engineers, assisting with cloud strategies, cloud migration planning, and design of cloud architecture at the bank.

AWS is not the only significant player in South Africa. Google, Microsoft, IBM, and Chinese cloud providers, Huawei and Alibaba, also have a market presence. Many of these global providers are

---

[20] Ibid.

[21] 'Cloud Computing Market 2023.' Research and Markets report.

offering training in different countries to develop talent as more business and governments shift to cloud computing. To increase gender diversity, all three companies offer programmes for women where they can develop specialized skills and get certified. For example, Google Cloud partnered with Women Techmakers by offering a certification journey for Ambassadors of the Women Techmakers community.[22] With support from a technical mentor, participants embark on a six week learning journey with access to Google Cloud's on-demand learning platform called Google Cloud Skills Boost.

The top cloud certifications, such as AWS Solutions Architect, Azure Fundamentals, and Google Associate Cloud Engineer, are in high demand and command higher salaries for those that are certified. In North America, the average salary difference between certified and non-certified IT staff was estimated to be 22 per cent. In the Asia-Pacific region, certified professionals were found to earn 45 per cent more than non-certified peers. Cloud certifications vary, catering to different roles and skill levels. Some certifications focus on foundational knowledge, while others teach advanced topics. There are also a number of non-profit organizations supporting women on this topic. The GirlCode is a non-profit organization providing cloud computing training through the SHE Dares Cloud Practitioner journey. The programme invites women all over South Africa to earn the Cloud Practitioner certification.[23] GirlCode CEO Zandile Mkhwanazi comments:

> Getting this certification means you can validate your cloud fluency with an industry-recognised credential from AWS and highlight your overall understanding of the AWS Cloud – with

---

[22] Magda Jary. 'Women Techmakers journey to Google Cloud certification'. *Google Cloud*. March 2022.

[23] 'Female cloud practitioners on the rise'. *ITWeb*. February 2023. https://www.itweb.co.za/content/PmxVEMKE3dxvQY85

our support every step of the way. If more organisations partner with us, we can get well on our way to ushering 10 million women into a tech career by 2030. It can only be accomplished when we come together as an industry.[24]

Several public and private partnerships have also emerged to encourage more women to learn about cloud computing. Women in Cloud, an international community-led economic development organization, aims to partner with 100 companies to create three new jobs per partner, resulting in 300 net new jobs for women. The organization collaborated with Microsoft to address the concern that only 14 per cent of cloud computing jobs were held by women. Women in Cloud found that technical certification, career development skills, and hands-on work experience were crucial factors for employment success.[25] 'Our first step was to provide access to Coursera Training and Microsoft Certification scholarships. Over the past 15 months, we have distributed over 3,000 scholarships to individuals across 65 countries.'[26]

Tinkering

'We will explore the mysteries of science and harness the power of technology and innovation. We will realise the opportunities of the digital world. Our youth will learn more from—and with—each other.'[27]

—Shri Narendra Modi, prime minister of India

---

[24] Ibid.

[25] Caroline Berrios. 'Bridging the gender gap: collective cloud apprentice program empowers women to break into the $7 trillion cloud computing industry'. *Women in Cloud.*August 2023.

[26] Ibid.

[27] *Beyond Tinkering: ATL Student Innovator Program Handbook.* Niti Aayog Atal Innovation Mission.

What happens if I press this button? What happens if I move it like this? Tinkering in the Oxford English Dictionary means 'attempt to repair or improve something in a casual or desultory way'.[28] Tinkering is the ability to take an item, take it apart, work out how to use it, and improve and experiment with it without any structure. It is described as a computational thinking approach to develop skills in critical thinking, collaboration, creativity, and communication. To train children with future skills, learning labs, classes, and books have been developed to encourage tinkering. It starts by inviting children to solve a problem. It could be as simple as building a boat that floats and holds pennies. Through tinkering, children figure out how materials and tools work, how to take things apart, and how to put things together. The benefits are that mistakes are expected. The children learn to accept them and learn from them.

Tinkering Labs have been introduced across schools in India. Schools now operate as part of a larger ecosystem. Some schools collaborate with each other, or have started to collaborate with other organizations in their communities, such as scientific organizations, technology companies, and businesses, where teachers and students learn about the skills and competencies that employers are seeking. With a national vision to 'cultivate one million children in India as Neoteric Innovators', the Government of India initiated the Atal Innovation Mission, partnering with digital companies. A key part of the initiative has been establishing Atal Tinkering Laboratories (ATLs). These labs were created in 10,000 schools benefitting approximately 7.5 million middle and high school students. ATLs introduce Indian students to a very different learning environment, which allows them the freedom to explore new ideas, test them, and follow a 'learning by doing' model. The ATL programme has become an Indian national

---

[28] Oxford Advanced Learner's Dictionary.

movement to implement an 'Experiential and Project-Based Learning' model as part of the country's education policy.

ATLs are making a difference to young girls and attracting them to STEM subjects. Together with Dell Technologies, ATLs launched the SheCodes Innovation Challenge in 2020. The programme encourages girls to tinker and to invent solutions in relation to agriculture, water conservation, waste management, clean energy, smart mobility, and health. The nationwide challenge reached out to 125,000 girls with the aim of accelerating their readiness to the future world of work. The programme was a success and by 2022, ShePreneur India was created with the same mission. Archana Sahay from Dell Technologies commented, 'So many of these products that these girls have come up with are products that solve day-to-day issues in their community.' By tinkering, Sahay, who started the impactful programme, says:

> We are seeing these girls driving the movement of change. And each one of them is creating their own path. Programs like Shepreneur are transforming education through technology and cultivating the inclusion of powering girls to learn and grow. And basically, they have a seat at the table, particularly in the STEM field.[29]

Shepreneur has encouraged 320 girls from across India to tinker and innovate with fifteen patents filed, and more than 300 prototypes launched.[30] Many of the innovations have already reached the commercial stage, each addressing a real-world problem that can change lives. For example, one girl invented an alert that prevents cattle from destroying crop fields by waking

---

[29] Sara Alvarez Kleinsmith 'Empowering girls to innovate, aspire and achieve'. *Dell Technologies*. March 2023.

[30] Ibid.

farmers and another invented a safety device that protects young women from being attacked while out alone. Two girls, Divyani Raut and Anjali Paunika, innovated an affordable and effective solution to address poor-quality drinking water in their village.[31] Together, the girls designed a real-time Water Quality Analysis System with sensors that rapidly read the water pollution, while IoT transfers data to the phones of the village leaders and district officials. According to Dell's Innovation Index, 56 per cent of innovation leaders polled in the global workforce are hosting hackathons and scrums to encourage innovation and collaborative problem-solving. With the Shepreneur programme, young girls are getting a head start.

Digital Leadership

'I think a good digital leader is someone who is able to inspire, to have a vision, to include digitalisation in his/her vision, and be able to share this with all employees.'[32]

—Cécile Bernheim, president, S2E Partners

Clara Waltz loved her job. She was good at it and had mastered her craft well. All those years studying computing were paying off. She was fast becoming the in-house expert that all the other graduates were going to for technical advice. At the end of the year, when she sat down for her appraisal, she walked into her boss' office with quiet confidence. She was smiling inside, and as she sat opposite the table looking at her boss, she patiently waited for him to say those magic words: You are promoted! Her boss did say those words, but only after he went through the appraisal

---

[31] Apurva P. 'Dell Technologies: Atal Tinkering Labs bring digital innovation to India's underserved communities'. *Social Story*. September 2022.

[32] Robert Mitson. 'Women in Digital: The obstacles and opportunities for an inclusive, digital world'. *Sherpany*.

form. Waltz was about to switch off when she heard the magic words. In her head, she was thinking, 'mission accomplished'. But there was more. 'In your new role, we would like to you to manage the other graduates.' Waltz's face dropped. She loved being the go-to-person, she loved the challenge of fixing people's problems. But she couldn't think of anything worse than managing others. Waltz was aspiring to be a technical leader. Technical leaders are responsible for making project-related or operational decisions (and have no direct reports), while people leaders manage people. These are distinct leadership roles, and being on the wrong leadership path could lead to career downfall.

As companies and organizations adopt a wide range of digital technologies, the distinction between technical and people leadership becomes more important. Some women leaders have the misconception that they must have all the technical skills to lead people in digital projects. This can put them off in applying for those leadership roles in tech-related organizations and industries where their people skills could be most valuable. This doesn't mean that people leaders in the technology field don't need to be digitally literate, quite the opposite. Leaders that are familiar with data and digital technologies and cyber threats are likely to be more successful. But what is more important is digital leadership. This type of leadership is the ability to utilize digital technology and data effectively in problem-solving, decision-making, and management. Sara Braund, vice president of digital operations at South32, is on point when she says:

> Technology is extremely broad and there are many roles that don't require deep technical expertise. Key skills are stakeholder management, the ability to communicate technical solutions to non-technical people and being able to influence and negotiate

well. Soft skills, such as communication, teamwork and problem solving are equally as important as technical skills.[33]

Similarly, Susan Wojcicki, the CEO of YouTube, said, 'Though we do need more women to graduate with technical degrees, I always like to remind women that you don't need to have science or technology degrees to build a career in tech.'[34] Kristen Nicole, editor of tech media company SiliconANGLE, echoes the same view, and that digital leadership can come in different forms. She says:

> There are so many women that already work with technology, even if they're not programmers or CIOs, that get overlooked in these discussions about women in tech. I know statisticians that have been crunching numbers for 20 years that should be applauded for their mastery of software in today's data science environments. I know women that work as project managers on large scale construction sites and head the implementation of Oracle software for an entire global office network that aren't counted as 'women in tech' because they work in what's traditionally considered a non-tech department.[35]

Women in digital leadership positions bring unique perspectives and ideas to the table. Their creativity and problem-solving abilities contribute to technological innovation and new solutions. But women tend to have fewer business-related connections than

---

[33] Pavel. 'How to break into the tech industry and create a rewarding career'. She Loves Data. September 2019. https://shelovesdata.com/2019/09/24/how-to-break-into-the-tech-industry-and-create-a-rewarding-career/

[34] 'Breaking barriers: top female innovators in tech.' *Apollo Solutions*. July 2023.

[35] Sean Allan. 'The Rise of Women in Tech: Will Thailand Reverse the Trend?' *Aware Technology Solutions for Business*. https://www.aware.co.th/rise-women-tech-will-thailand-reverse-trend/

men. Women often have a fear of networking, yet they must build work relationships. Women supporting other women is key to more women succeeding in business, particularly in leadership roles. Many women in digital leadership are involved in building and supporting networks and communities for women by providing resources, mentoring, and creating a sense of belonging.

Women in digital leadership can also shape digital policies and regulations, ensuring that they consider gender-specific and ethical concerns. Women are excelling in the area of ethics. Overall, women have been found to be less tolerant than men of a wide array of unethical negotiating strategies. A study found that 25 per cent of men used deception to negotiate a deal, as compared with only 11 per cent of women.[36] New roles in ethics are emerging and compared to men, more women are holding these senior positions.

Unfortunately, women hold only 14 per cent of leadership roles in technology.[37] The presence of women in digital leadership is essential for ensuring that the technology sector reflects the diversity of society and addresses the challenges and opportunities that women face. Encouraging and supporting women in digital leadership positions contributes to a more inclusive and innovative digital world. There are eight different superpowers that women can tap into to develop stronger interpersonal and digital leadership skills—**collaboration, empathy, intuition, optimism, patience, management,** and **organizational**. Many of these are displayed by Shuri, the Black Panther! If these skills were to be recognized by employers by a greater extent, there is scope for more women to be employed in digital jobs. Joseph Fuller, who co-leads Harvard Business School's Managing the Future of

---

[36] Katie Shonk. 'Moral Leadership: Do Women Negotiate More Ethically than Men?' *Harvard Law School*. November 2023.

[37] Maria Webb. '60+ Women in Tech Statistics You Need to Know in 2024: Trends, Gaps, and Challenges'. *Technopedia*. March 2024.

Work research programme, says that new technology will allow women to overcome skills gaps that prevent them entering many male-dominated professions.[38] A skills-first approach to hiring in male-dominated jobs could increase the pool of potential female talent by eight-fold. Fuller says that women, who generally have 'superior social skills', will disproportionately benefit.

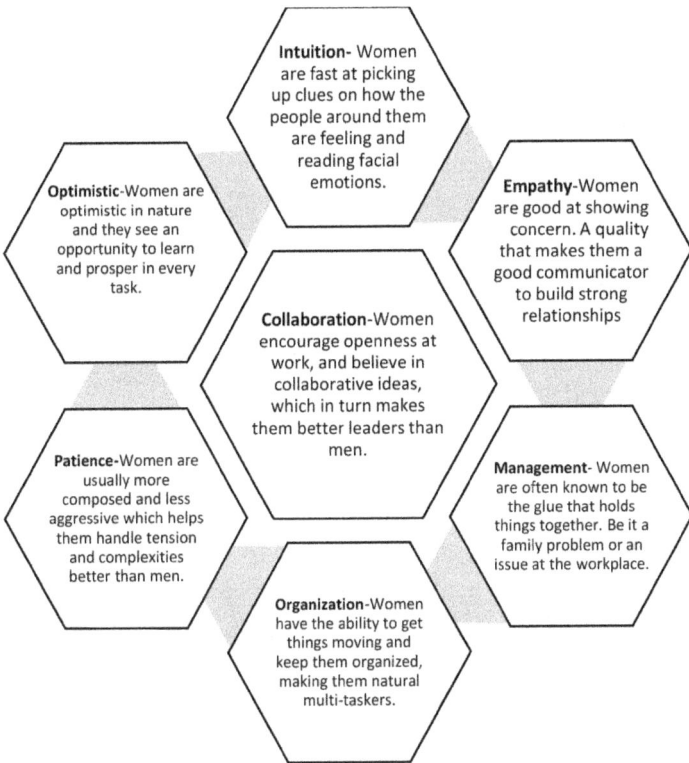

Figure 1: Superpowers for the Future[39]

[38] Amy Borrett. 'New tech is both a threat and a benefit for women's access to work'. *The Financial Times*. October 2023.

[39] 'The Superpowers of (Super)women: The Most Powerful Strengths of Women'. *Medium*. 2015.

Southeast Asia's Female Tech Workforce

'As a woman, I look forward to witnessing more female leaders in tech in the future. At SEA (Thailand), we actively foster an inclusive and supportive corporate culture to facilitate the career advancement of female talent.'[40]

—Maneerut Anulomsombut, CEO, SEA (Thailand)

Technology companies in Southeast Asia have a strong track record of hiring women. Thailand leads the way with 42 per cent of the technology workforce being female, with Singapore close behind at 41 per cent. The region's digital economies are growing, benefitting from the rise in women working in the technology sector. In 2023, the Southeast Asian digital economy delivered $100 billion in revenue, growing at 27 per cent CAGR since 2021, 1.7 times faster than gross merchandise value (GMV).[41] The government's support for training women in the region is commendable, although further work is required to increase women in senior roles.[42]

Singapore's digital economy has been attracting women from different backgrounds, including women from non-technology backgrounds. The government's investment in growing the female workforce is paying off with more initiatives being introduced. Mrs Josephine Teo, the minister for communications and information and minister-in-charge of smart nation and cybersecurity, has been a role model in actively championing

---

[40] Suchit Leesa-nguansuk. 'Leading by example'. *The Bangkok Post*. June 2023. https://www.bangkokpost.com/business/general/2600243/leading-by-example

[41] Florian Hoppe, Aadarsh Baijal, Willy Chang, Sapna Chadna, and Fock Wai Hoong. 'e-Conomy SEA 2023. Reaching new heights: Navigating the path to profitable growth'. *Bain & Company*. November 2023.

[42] Vaishali Rastogi, Michael Meyer, Michael Tan, and Justine Tasiaux. 'Boosting Women in Technology in Southeast Asia'. October 2020.

women and leading the government's efforts to digitally upskill women.[43] She is a strong advocate for women stating that, 'Women possess the skills to succeed in the overlapping fields of AI and cyber security that are in their nascent stage'.[44] Minister Teo launched the SG Women in Tech (SGWiT), an initiative focused on attracting, inspiring, and encouraging women to pursue careers in the technology sector.[45] In 2021, SGWiT successfully led a Corporate Pledge where over fifty companies agreed to create a conducive environment for existing women tech professionals, as well as to encourage more young women to join the field.[46] Some of these pledges include rolling out mentorships, employee-led support groups, webinars, and even coding workshops for young female students to spark their interest in the exciting world of digital technology.

Singapore's share of women in STEM jobs has increased from around 30 per cent in 2015 to 32 per cent in 2020, but the government wants more women to pursue careers in these fields. In early 2022, the government set a goal to empower and mentor 3,000 aspiring women by end of 2023 under the Ladies in Cyber Charter.[47] The government surpassed its goal. Training in cybersecurity continued and the Cyber Security Agency of Singapore announced 10,000 training opportunities for women to develop essential cybersecurity skills.

In Thailand, the first female managing director of Hewlett Packard commented that Southeast Asia has a strong history of

---

[43] Prime Minister's Office Singapore, Mrs Josephine Teo.

[44] Samuel Devaraj. 'Women possess skills to succeed in AI and cyber security: Josephine Teo.' *The Straits Times*. March 2023.

[45] Jill Arul. 'Breaking down barriers: Women supporting women in tech'. *Infocomm Media Development Authority*. October 2021.

[46] Ibid.

[47] Samuel Devaraj. 'Women possess skills to succeed in AI and cyber security: Josephine Teo.' *The Straits Times*. March 2023.

hiring women and recognizes that promoting gender diversity will deliver significant benefits. Over half of Thailand's population and social media users are women, and so female representation becomes a no-brainer to meet customer needs. Katherine Aphaivongs, who runs a financial comparison portal, has noticed the shift in Thailand. 'Women are beginning to turn towards the tech industry more as the market begins to mature. As with any industry, there needs to be a demand.'[48]

Jirakorn 'Dew' Nai Fun has been working with Aware for the past eleven years, a company focused on Business-to-Business (B2B) applications that removes redundant manual processes and drive down costs. Dew works as a business analyst.[49] She studied industrial engineering at Chiang Mai University at a time when engineering faculties all over Thailand were populated mostly by men. She spoke about the past when 'women only studied in the nursing or teaching fields'. Now she says that has changed, and that Thai women study in a variety of fields. 'When I studied engineering, I think only 10% of the students were women, but now I think it's almost equal. Gender doesn't make such a difference anymore.'[50]

Thai women are also inspiring other women in the country, including those that work within government. Theresa Mathawaphan, chief strategy officer, National Innovation Agency (NIA), Thailand, says, 'My mentors are the senior colleagues and advisors that I've worked with, especially female leaders. They are my inspirations for being strong minded, smart and independent women, with good ethics and integrity.'[51] NIA is a national

[48] Vaishali Rastogi, Michael Meyer, Michael Tan, and Justine Tasiaux. 'Boosting Women in Technology in Southeast Asia'. October 2020.

[49] Sean Allan. 'The Rise of Women in Tech: Will Thailand Reverse the Trend?' *Aware Technology Solutions for Business.*

[50] Ibid.

[51] Yun Xuan Poon. 'Theresa Mathawaphan, chief strategy officer, National Innovation Agency Thailand'. *Gov Insider.* December 2021.

agency tasked with building the innovation capability of Thailand. Mathawaphan shares:

> I have seen that the innovation policy is starting to pick up in its momentum in Thailand. 2022 will be the year that we can push further the innovation policy to a higher level, at the Prime Minister level and the Ministry level. Driving the awareness of GII (Global Innovation Index) in Thailand and laying ground work of measures for sending the country to higher position through technology and innovation.[52]

Inspiring Māori Women

> 'Tūpuna were innovators, explorers, and discoverers and so we should really just tap into that side of ourselves and go out and be willing to learn.'[53]
> —Aleisha Amohia of Te Āti Haunui a Pāpārangi

'I'm still very much a minority as a young brown woman in the tech industry,' says Aleisha Amohi (Te Āti Haunui a Pāpārangi), a Māori leading the National Council of Women of New Zealand in Wellington. Around 17 per cent of New Zealand's population are reported to be Māori, an ethnicity which originates from settlers from East Polynesia. But Māori and Pasifika employees are underrepresented across New Zealand's digital economy, only accounting for 5.2 per cent and 6.7 per cent of Auckland's

---

[52] Yun Xuan Poon. 'Theresa Mathawaphan, chief strategy officer, National Innovation Agency Thailand'. *Gov Insider*. December 2021.

[53] Kahumako Rameka. 'Māori wahine in pursuit of excellence in the technology world, led by her ancestors'. *Te ao Māori News*. July 2022. https://www.teaonews. co.nz/2022/07/15/maori-wahine-in-pursuit-of-excellence-in-the-technology-world-led-by-her-ancestors/

technology workforce.[54] Despite being a minority, Amohia urges the younger generation (*rangatahi* in Māori) interested in technology to let the example left by ancestors guide them. 'That's what kind of gets me up is knowing that the work that I'm doing and the work that the organisations I belong to are doing is hopefully going to shape a future where young girls don't have to wake up and feel different.'[55] Amohia was fifteen when she first became interested in technology. After studying a science degree in AI, she became a program developer and now represents the Māori voice within InternetNZ. A specialist Māori Design Group was established to support InternetNZ deepen its understanding of Te Ao Māori and improve Māori relationships and outcomes. Amohia co-leads the group, sharing her experience in technology and community.[56]

Maru Nihoniho, the founder and managing director of Metia Interactive, said that one solution to increase representation was for New Zealand tech businesses to collaborate with schools and develop a system where Māori children could become interested in creative technologies.[57] She also recommended inspiring students through gaming. 'When we started releasing games inspired by Māori stories, we found that our young people loved them'.[58] Inspiring the younger generation alone is not enough. The Māori community can benefit significantly from the fourth industrial revolution and there is a need to raise the awareness

---

[54] Mildred Armah. 'Māori, Pasifika and women under-represented in Auckland's tech industry'. *Stuff News*. June 2022. https://www.stuff.co.nz/technology/129000126/mori-pasifika-and-women-underrepresented-in-aucklands-tech-industry

[55] Ibid, 137.

[56] Megan. 'New Māori Design Group to help InternetNZ create better outcomes for Māori'. *InternetNZ*. November 2021. https://internetnz.nz/news-and-articles/new-maori-design-group-to-help-internetnz-create-better-outcomes-for-maori/

[57] Ibid, 137.

[58] Ibid.

of the opportunities on offer. For example, a young Māori woman wanted to pursue a career in technology. She could see opportunities. However, her parents didn't understand the careers available in the technology sector. They wanted her to be a lawyer or teacher as they were common and reputable professions. Undeterred, she set up a community, to educate others and to be a role model so that other Māori could identify with her.

Other organizations have also been inspiring Māori women. She Sharp, a non-profit organization that supports women in STEM, hosted their first ever conference Inspire Her, for Māori and Pasifika girls in years 11-13. At the conference, over 100 students had the opportunity to participate in hands-on workshops in robotics, AI, VR and AR.[59] Companies like Fonterra, a dairy multinational, and MYOB, which provides business software, showcased STEM career paths and the Auckland University of Technology. Keen to inspire these girls, some teachers drove for two hours to bring girls from remote locations to the Auckland event.

Another game changer is the online platform developed by Innovative Young Minds (IYM).[60] Delivered with the telecommunication company Chorus, IYM Online 2024 is open to young women. The programme is entirely online, and participants are exposed to a wide range of research and career opportunities. IYM provides one-on-one mentoring, creates networking opportunities, and showcases profiles of women who have achieved success.[61] The platform provides virtual

---

[59] 'Inspire Her: te whakatipuranga wahine'. *She Sharp*. https://www.shesharp. org.nz/events/inspire-her-te-whakatipuranga-wahine

[60] Innovative Young Minds website: https://www.iym.org.nz/

[61] Ripu Bhatia. 'Online platform aims to guide young women into science and technology careers'. *Stuff News*. September 2023. https://www.stuff.co.nz/pou-tiaki/133009819/online-platform-aims-to-guide-young-women-into-science-and-technology-careers

tours of laboratories and other spaces in universities, as well as team-building and networking sessions using digital technology.

> **What digital skills do women need?**

> Women have many skills—you can think of them as superpowers. These superpowers are vital for the digital economy. To stay ahead, young girls and women need to learn and develop skills for the digital revolution. This could be learning to code, getting young girls to tinker, and attracting women to have the courage to lead in the digital economy. While women must invest in themselves, they need support—from men, from companies, from governments, and from investors.

Chapter 7

Men and the Revolution

'By participating in the movement to empower women in tech, men can at least make the gap smaller.'[1]
—Pauls Silins, project director, Riga TechGirls

Taylor Swift was named *Time* magazine's Person of the Year in 2023. Every year, the prestigious award goes to an event or a person deemed to have had the most influence on global events over the past year, like former US presidents and the Queen of England. Swift, estimated to have a net worth of $1.1billion, described the moment as 'the proudest and happiest I've ever felt'.[2] Swift spent 2023 travelling the world on her 'Eras Tour', 'showcasing music from her entire career, smashing records for ticket sales, and boosting the economies of every city she visited', reports Reuters. The tour made around $900 million of revenue in 2023.[3] With fans ranging from eight to eighty years old, Sam Jacobs, the *Time*'s editor-in chief said that Swift was 'the rare person who is both the writer and hero of her own story . . .

---

[1] Tony Fyler. 'Women in tech: how men can help'. *Women in Tech*. September 2023.

[2] 'Taylor Swift named Time's Person of the Year, capping her record-breaking 2023'. *Reuters*. December 2023.

[3] Ibid.

[she] found a way to transcend borders and be a source of light'.[4] Jacobs is the youngest male editor the magazine has had since its co-founder Henry Luce.[5] His passion for telling stories that shape the world and shining the light on female changemakers is very much needed, more so in relation to our digital economy. For example, in the same week that Swift was voted *Time's* Person of the Year, another prominent American media publisher printed the top people in the AI field. The internationally known *New York Times* listed 'who's who' in the Modern Artificial Intelligence Movement.[6] However, for some, the list was a source of frustration rather than inspiration. Why? The list of twelve experts featured no women.[7] Disappointed journalists and academics listed all the potential female AI experts that could have been named. Sasha Luccioni, a researcher at the AI community Hugging Face, said, 'Apparently it's ok to include "an internet philosopher and self-taught A.I. researcher" and . . . Musk of all people? But not women who actually made massive contributions to the field, from Fei-Fei Li to Doina Precup and Joelle Pineau.'[8] Even Dr Li herself commented, 'It's not about me, but all of us in AI, all of the incredible "godmothers", pioneers, active researchers, students from all walks of life.'[9] With AI becoming so prevalent in our daily lives, whether it's work or social, the *New York Times* had the opportunity to showcase female

---

[4] Sam Jacobs. '2023 The Choice: Taylor Swift.' *TIME Magazine*. December 2023.

[5] 'Sam Jacobs Named Editor in Chief of TIME.' *Time Magazine*. April 2023.

[6] J. Edward Moreno. 'Who's Who behind the Dawn of the Modern Artificial Intelligence Movement'. *The New York Times*. December 2023.

[7] Kai Xiang Teo. AI Experts are roasting the NYT list of 'who's who" in AI for having zero women. *The Business Insider*. December 2023.

[8] Ibid.

[9] Fei-Fei Li (@drfeifei). *X*. 3 December 2023. https://x.com/drfeifei/status/1731369148654260406

role models to future generations. They had the opportunity to show the world that the female digital revolution is happening.

The omission from the *New York Times* list was also criticized by male experts. Technology investor Vinod Khosla said that he was a huge fan of Dr Li and thought that the list was poorly thought through.[10] Toby Walsh, chief scientist at Australia's University of New South Wales AI Institute was also not impressed. 'Next time, include some of the academics who came up with the ideas now being implemented. And make the list more diverse, some women perhaps?'[11] Having men speak up for these missed opportunities speaks volumes. In the digital economy, male support is vital for the future success of the female digital revolution. Without their support as leaders, colleagues, husbands, fathers, brothers, the full economic and social benefits of digital technology cannot be achieved. So how exactly can men help? In the next section, we take a look at how the role of men in our society and economy has changed over the decades. In Chapter one we sought to understand the changing role of women; we must also then do the same for men. It is only then can we provide recommendations on how men can support women in the digital economy.

The Changing Role of Men

'The dynamic engagement of women will also enrich men's lives.'[12]

—Shinzo Abe, former prime minister of Japan

---

[10] Vinod Khosla (@vkhosla). *X.* 4 December 2023. https://x.com/vkhosla/status/1731450091884696046

[11] Toby Walsh (@TobyWalsh). *X.* 4 December 2023. https://x.com/TobyWalsh/status/1731511439960260760

[12] Opening Speech by Prime Minister Shinzo Abe at the Open Forum, World Assembly for Women in Tokyo: WAW! 2015. https://www.mofa.go.jp/files/000096924.pdf

In the first chapter, we found that industrial revolutions changed the role of women. The same is true for the role of men. The Second Industrial Revolution in the 1900s changed men's lives as they migrated from rural areas and farming jobs to urban centres with factory jobs. As primary breadwinners of the time, men moved their families to areas with better employment in emerging industries. Working in factories meant that men often worked long hours, which meant that they spent very little time at home. Women, if they worked, took on jobs within the home while caring for children. Now, the jobs undertaken by men have changed, and so has their family life. Men are increasingly seeking a balance between work and personal life, seeking flexible work arrangements and paternity leave. Research shows that working men are now spending significantly more time per workday with their children than they did in the 1970s.[13] Modern fathers spend an average of 4.1 hours with their children under the age of thirteen on workdays, up from two hours in 1977.[14] Men are also seeking professions beyond traditionally male-dominated fields, such as nursing, teaching, and administrative roles.

Despite these changes, men continue to dominate leadership positions in many industries and start-ups in the digital economy, although there's a growing recognition of the need for diversity and inclusion. Men continue to be paid more than women as their confidence often translates to better jobs with better pay. A study found that men were able to negotiate entry-level salaries 7.6 per cent higher than women. Where only 7 per cent of women were able to negotiate for more money, more than 50 per cent of men did the same. But men, just like women, are facing challenges that could affect their participation in the digital economy. Men and

[13] 'Fathers spend seven times more with their children than in the 1970s.' *The Guardian.* 2014.

[14] LinkedIn post by Neo Mpele. 'Stereotypes Men Face.' November 2019. https://www.linkedin.com/pulse/stereotypes-men-face-neo-mpele

even young boys are sometimes punished when they step outside of masculine norms. One collection of studies showed that 'men face backlash when they don't adhere to masculine gender stereotypes—when they show vulnerability, act nicer, display empathy, express sadness, exhibit modesty, and proclaim to be feminists.'[15] Men who do this tend to earn less, get promoted less often, and overall receive worse performance reviews than women who engage in similar behaviour. Some organizations view commitment to the job and always being available as an indicator of someone's value to the organization. For some men, work conflicts with outside-of-work commitments. Former Prime Minister Shinzo Abe sought to change this as part of his Womenomics strategy.

> [O]ur greatest barrier is a working culture that endorses male-centered long working hours. If men themselves do not awaken to this fact and take action, we will not be able to eliminate this bad practice. First of all, we will expand a corporate culture that values working efficiently within a limited number of hours. Husbands will also actively take childcare leave and couples will share responsibility for household chores and child rearing. We will make this the ordinary practice in Japan.[16]

It is not just high-powered officials that hold this view. Men working in the digital economy also feel that men need to change, as one man working for a technology consulting firm shared that 'Men need help too, so that they can support their partners.'[17]

---

[15] David Mayer. 'How men get penalized for straying from masculine norms.' October 2018.

[16] Opening Speech by Prime Minister Shinzo Abe at the Open Forum, World Assembly for Women in Tokyo: WAW! 2015. https://www.mofa.go.jp/files/000096924.pdf

[17] Nimisha Tailor. Interview with AI Consultant. July 2023.

Some men have recognized the gender imbalance and are making it their mission to support, train, and mentor women into digital jobs. These are men leading companies, start-ups, venture capitalists, government agencies, or non-profit organizations. For example, Japan's minister, Masanobu Ogura, recognizes that Japan still has a gender problem. Ogura is the only male gender equality minister among the Group of Seven nations (G-7). 'The "digital gap" was a shared challenge among all G-7 members at our meeting last year. Women only make up 19 per cent of those working in the digital sphere in Japan, and there are few female role models in the technology industry.'[18] Male business leaders are making sure that credit is given where credit is due. For instance, Satya Nadella, the chief executive of Microsoft and a shareholder in OpenAI, pointed out that when the CEO was temporarily fired, Murati, the company's CTO, demonstrated an ability to assemble teams with technical expertise, commercial acumen, and a deep appreciation for the importance of mission.[19] In his praise he stated that, 'Mira has helped build some of the most exciting AI technologies we've ever seen.'

These are just some examples of how influential men are recognizing the contributions of women in designing technology and speaking out in favour of increasing women's participation in the digital economy. Not only is it imperative for our digital society, but it also makes economic sense. The Australian Computer Society Digital Pulse report warned that if no action is taken, the lack of women in technology could cost the country $7.27 billion over the next twenty years.[20] Singapore estimates that reaching an equal number of women-owned businesses

---

[18] Alice French, Rurika Imahashi, and Wataru Suzuki. 'Inside Japan's gender problem: The men tasked with empowering women'. *Nikkei Asia*. January 2023.

[19] Lauren Aratani. 'How OpenAI interim chief Mira Murati helped launch AI into the mainstream'. *The Guardian*. November 2023.

[20] Kathryn Lewis. 'Failure to boost women in tech could cost economy $11b over 20 years'. *The Canberra Times*. June 2021.

and men-owned businesses could add $70 billion to Singapore's economy—roughly 20 per cent of GDP.[21] How do we get there? How do these figures become reality? Below are some specific suggestions on how men can support women either at home or in the workplace.

Sponsor (and Mentor) Women in the Workplace

'I am proud to be working in a company with such a strong female representation, and sponsorship at all levels with our CEO setting the tone from the top.'[22]

—Harini Gokul, chief customer officer, Entrust

Many men already understand the benefits of diversity and the skills and perspectives that women bring to the workplace. These nurturing men are voluntarily mentoring and training female talent. They have taken it upon themselves to be cheerleaders for the women they work with. Much of this support is not noticed or spoken about enough. In other cases, more effort is required. A key concern, from interviews, is that not enough men are sponsoring or mentoring women in the workplace, leaving women disheartened when their careers don't progress while watching their male colleagues rapidly advance.

A mentor is typically someone who provides guidance, advice, and support to a mentee based on their own experiences and expertise. On the other hand, a sponsor is someone who actively advocates for and supports the career advancement of an individual within an organization or professional context. Both roles are important for professional development and can play a big part in a woman's professional life. But they serve different functions. Let me explain further.

---

[21] 'Businesswomen Grow Economies: Singapore is Next'. *Accenture*. 2015.

[22] Harini Gokul. 'Women get mentors, men get sponsors'. *TechUk*. March 2023.

Research suggests that 71 per cent of sponsors are the same gender or race as their primary protégés, which hinders scope for inclusive workplaces.[23] Although having a female sponsor may be more comfortable for women, these senior women are limited in supply in male-dominated environments. In these situations, which are common in companies involved in developing technology or implementing digital transformations, having more men sponsoring women can increase their visibility within the organization and support networking. For example, former Facebook and Visa chief marketing officer, Antonio Lucio, has been sponsoring many women. He has encouraged women to rethink their beliefs around organizational politics and power, and focus on networking, making strong connections, and taking on high-profile projects.[24] Peter Grauer, chairman of the board of Bloomberg L.P., has also been sponsoring women, but describes his first experience as difficult in convincing others that his protégé was capable.[25] If more men take on a sponsoring role, these challenges could soon disappear. Samantha Ross Saperstein, global head of Women on the Move at JPMorgan Chase, advises men to consider sponsorship as part of the onboarding process when a woman joins their team. 'In addition to ensuring they have all the information they need to do the job, also make sure they have the right people in their corner from the beginning.'[26]

Similarly, there is scope for men to mentor women as part of their personal and professional development. David Smith, PhD,

---

[23] The Sponsor Dividend. *Centre for Talent Innovation* (now *Coqual*). 2019.

[24] Samantha Ross Saperstein. 'Why More Men Should Become Sponsors for Women'. *Time*. August 2023.

[25] Vivian Giang. 'The male leaders committed to sponsoring women'. *Fast Company*. May 2019. https://www.fastcompany.com/90335152/the-male-leaders-committed-to-sponsoring-women

[26] Samantha Ross Saperstein. 'Why More Men Should Become Sponsors for Women'. *Time*. August 2023.

author of *Athena Rising: How and Why Men Should Mentor Women*, explains that both men and women can benefit from mentoring:[27]

> Women get more raises, they advance faster, and they stay in the organization longer. That's not because men are better mentors, but because they have positions of influence and power. Men get increased access to information, they build a more diverse and expansive network, and they tend to increase their interpersonal skills.

It is also important to mentor in a way that best suits the mentee. For instance, a vice president of Goldman Sachs was known for having a breakfast/lunch-only policy for mentoring because women felt more comfortable with that approach.[28] In Singapore, women's community networks have invited C-suite men to participate in mentoring walks. Described as 'Walk the talk', the event pairs 100 of Singapore and Asia's men with 200–300 early and mid-career women for a morning walk to discuss the real challenges women face at work.[29] Assaf Tarnopolsky, former general manager in a cloud computing company, said that participating in the mentor walk was a no brainer.[30] He believes in being a mensch—a person of integrity with a sense of what is right and responsible—and the community event made it easy to provide different female professionals with insightful advice. For example, at the start of the walk, he advised a female to highlight her transferrable skills rather than her company identity, if she wanted to change her career to another industry.

---

[27] Fiona Macaulay. 'The Surprising Benefits When Men Mentor Women'. *Inc.* 2019.

[28] Ibid.

[29] Walk the Talk 2024. https://www.eventbrite.sg/e/walk-the-talk-2024-tickets-824888272027

[30] Nimisha Tailor. Interview with Assaf Tarnopolsky. April 2024.

Advocate for Women

> 'Achieving gender equality requires the engagement of women and men, girls and boys. It is everyone's responsibility.'[31]
> —Ban Ki-Moon, former secretary general of United Nations

Men and boys who grow up seeing equal relationships between their parents are more likely to be equal themselves. This can translate to greater support for the women in their lives, like wives pivoting to new roles involving technology like AI, cybersecurity, or data science, or mothers returning to work after a career break, or daughters investing in learning new digital skills.

For women to succeed, they need equality at home, ranging from childcare to household chores. This also relates to office admin at the workplace. 'The person taking diligent notes in the meeting almost never makes the killer point.'[32] Yale professor Victoria L. Brescoll's study found that women not only speak less often than men in meetings, but when male executives speak more than their peers, they are rewarded with 10 per cent higher competence ratings.[33] Hence, the advice here is don't assign women duties like note taking at meetings, organizing office parties, or training new hires.[34] This is particularly important if we want women to have a voice in designing technologies or developing algorithms, digital policies, or managing digital transformation within our organizations. At work, men can

---

[31] 'Secretary-General's remarks to closing session of high-level event of the General Assembly "The contributions of women, the young and civil society to the post-2015 development agenda"'. *United Nations*. March 2014.

[32] Adam Grant and Sheryl Sandberg. 'Madam C.E.O., Get Me a Coffee'. *New York Times*. February 2015.

[33] 'Here's How to Actually Support Women at Work'. *Create & Cultivate*. October 2016. https://www.createcultivate.com/blog/2016/11/22/men-heres-how-to-actually-support-women-at-work

[34] Lynn Cavanaugh. 'The Power of the Male Ally: Engaging Men, Advancing Women'. *Progressive Women's Leadership*. October 2016.

be powerful allies by acknowledging and celebrating women's contributions publicly and taking the time to educate themselves about unconscious bias and privilege. One courageous male leader in the area of digital finance did just that. He attended women's networking events to understand the gender gap. Similarly, some men have been aware of their own privileges and have refused to participate in conferences or panel discussions where there are no women presenting. For example, so far, over 100 men have signed a pledge to challenge the prevalence of all-male panels, or "manels", in conferences, events, and discussions as part of an initiative led by the Association for Women in Cryptocurrency.[35]

Men can also advocate for family-friendly policies, flexible work arrangements, and parental leave policies that support all employees. A male digital consultant pointed out that these initiatives would benefit men, too, in getting greater work-life balance.

> What is the role of men in the female digital revolution?

> Men must not be forgotten in this revolution. While their role is changing too, they can support women in ways that can accelerate their education, career paths, and incomes, benefitting the whole of society. Men can use their positions of power, visibility, and influence to give women a voice at home, work, and in our communities and countries. We encourage men to use current and emerging technology to innovate for women, invest in women, and become mentors and sponsors for a vibrant digital economy.

---

[35] Amanda Wicks on LinkedIn: https://www.linkedin.com/posts/amandawick_unmanelyourpanel-activity-7189321126760603649-dF6Q/

Chapter 8

Riding the Revolution

'When digital transformation is done right, it's like a caterpillar turning into a butterfly, but when done wrong, all you have is a really fast caterpillar.'[1]

—George Westerman, principal research scientist,
MIT Sloan Initiative on Digital Economy

In earlier chapters, we identified the missed opportunities, and we outlined the power of women as digital economic agents and the role of men. The most important discussion of all is what happens next. What actions are needed? Digitalization is everywhere all at once, whether you like it or not. It's everyone's job to make it inclusive. There is no silver bullet but a collection of strategies that requires all of us to think bigger. It requires companies to support women in the workplace and government to develop more inclusive policies, and investors and innovators to innovate and cater to women's needs. How exactly can investors, entrepreneurs, businesses, and government leaders (of all genders) be part of the female digital revolution? Here we take the time to provide a number of recommendations on how each of these agents can ride the revolution.

---

[1] Howard Rosen. 'Digital Transformation Isn't Just About Bits And Bytes—It's About People'. *Forbes*. March 2022.

What Can Companies Do?

'Working with and investing in women is one of the most powerful ways to spur sustainable economic growth and development.'[2]

—Muhtar Kent, CEO, The Coca-Cola Company

Women in the digital economy are missing out on good quality jobs and higher pay. Companies are also missing out on skilled and productive workers that can help them keep pace with technological advancement. To seize the opportunities, companies need to prioritize and value diversity, particularly by actively including more women in their teams. As new businesses emerge in the digital economy, new companies can move away from old biases. One company that seems to be doing things right is Cisco, which was voted one of the best workplaces for men and women in 2023, in the US.[3] Cisco, a global technology company developing telecommunications equipment, has won the number one spot for the third consecutive year. In Singapore, the company ranked number one in the country's Best Workplaces in the Medium Category in 2022.[4] Olivia G, a leader in strategy and planning, says:

> The company emphasizes diversity, equity, and inclusion by hiring diverse talent and spotlighting its inclusive communities like Women of Cisco and Conexion to connect them! I have benefited from participating in numerous networking events,

---

[2] 'The Coca-Cola Company Expands 5by20 Women's Economic Empowerment Initiative.' The Coca-Cola Company. November 2012.

[3] Cisco. *Great Place to Work*. August 2023.

[4] 'The Number 1 Best Workplace And Best In Technology'. *CIO World Asia*. November 2022.

personal and professional development programs, and volunteer and mentorship opportunities at Cisco or through Cisco. I am a proud first-generation Mexican American woman and have learned so much about myself and the benefits I bring to my everyday life by leading with who I am.[5]

With a happy workforce, Cisco has a strong global brand advocating for women. It was appointed by FIFA as the Official Network Infrastructure Provider for the Women's World Cup 2023 in Australia and New Zealand, where they provided the technology to host games in nine cities and ten stadiums.[6]

One way that companies can be more gender inclusive is by being clear on its mission and adopting the UN's Women Empowerment Principles (WEP)[7], which were developed using real-life business practices from across the globe. For instance, companies like Telefónica, a Spanish multinational telecommunications company, and Everphone, a company that manages mobile devices for organizations, have adopted the UN's Principles, as well as companies in other parts of the world.[8]

---

[5] Kathleen Loescher. Cisco Is #1 on Fortune's 100 Best Companies to Work For. In the U.S. List—Again!'. *Cisco*. April 2023. https://blogs.cisco.com/wearecisco/cisco-is-1-on-fortunes-100-best-companies-to-work-for-in-the-u-s-list-again

[6] 'Cisco joins FIFA Women's World Cup 2023 as Official Network Infrastructure Provider'. *Fédération Internationale de Football Association (FIFA)*. April 2023.

[7] 'Women's Empowerment Principles'. *UN Women Asia Pacific*. https://asiapacific.unwomen.org/sites/default/files/Field%20Office%20ESEAsia/Docs/Publications/2016/05/WEP-Booklet-en.pdf

[8] Telefónica website: https://www.telefonica.com/en/ Everphone website: https://everphone.com/en/

Intellias is the first Ukrainian IT company to adopt WEP,[9] and in China, since July 2019, forty-four CEOs signed up too.[10]

Other measures that businesses can introduce include offering flexible and remote work, hiring women at all levels, and having a targeted approach to recruiting women. The next section explains how these measures can make a difference.

UN's Women Empowerment Principles[11]

- Principle 1: Establish high-level corporate leadership for gender equality.
- Principle 2: Treat all women and men fairly at work—respect and support human rights and non-discrimination.
- Principle 3: Ensure the health, safety, and well-being of all women and men workers.
- Principle 4: Promote education, training, and professional development for women.
- Principle 5: Implement enterprise development, supply chain, and marketing practices that empower women.
- Principle 6: Promote equality through community initiatives and advocacy.
- Principle 7: Measure and publicly report on progress to achieve gender equality.

---

[9] Intellias website: https://intellias.com/

[10] Lin Jialei and Liu Di. 'China's companies step up support for Women's Empowerment Principles'. UN *Women Asia Pacific*. March 2020.

[11] 'Women's Empowerment Principles'. UN *Women Asia Pacific*. https://asiapacific.unwomen.org/sites/default/files/Field%20Office%20ESEAsia/Docs/Publications/2016/05/WEP-Booklet-en.pdf

Offer Flexible and Remote Work

'The firm, given the incentives, can always find a way to have
good substitutes.'[12]

—Professor Claudia Goldin, Nobel Prize winner for
Economic Sciences

There is scope for more companies to offer women (and
men) flexible and remote work in many different professions.
Claudia Goldin's economic research led her to discover that the
highest-paying jobs today require employees to work on evenings
and weekends, often on an unpredictable schedule.[13] In such jobs,
'doubling the number of hours more than doubles the earnings',
and often leads to promotion.[14] Goldin describes these as 'time-
greedy jobs' which are dominated by men, often enabled by
wives who handle the home front. However, Goldin argues that
managerial innovation could allow employees to substitute for each
other to make these jobs more mother-friendly. Goldin found that
women's wages increase when the work is redesigned to offer both
flexibility and substitutability. Her example is pharmacists. When
more pharmacies were independent, the pharmacist had to always
be on call, and most pharmacists were men. But the rise of chain
stores meant that pharmacists could work in shifts and substitute
for each other as needed. These days, pharmacists in the US have
one of the smallest gender-wage gaps among high-earning fields.
It's also a profession that's now majority female.

Compared to before, flexible and remote work has become
common, as it became necessary during the Covid-19 pandemic.

---

12 'If We Want Equity, Work Needs to Be Less Greedy.' Podcast *Women at
Work*, Season 7, Episode 5. *Harvard Business Review*. November 2021.

13 Claudia Goldin. *Career and Family: Women's Century-Long Journey toward Equity*.

14 'If We Want Equity, Work Needs to Be Less Greedy.' Podcast *Women at
Work*, Season 7, Episode 5. *Harvard Business Review*. November 2021.

However, with the pandemic over, some employees have been asked to come back to the office. In these situations, people have been resistant, demanding that remote work needs to stay, or they will quit. In fact, many did just that during the Covid-19 outbreak. The pandemic led some workers to re-evaluate life priorities and reduce working hours, or leave the job market entirely. It was known as the 'Great Resignation', starting in the US, as large numbers of employees voluntarily resigned from their jobs in early 2021. Inflexible remote-work policies were among the reasons for resigning, as well as poor wage growth amid rising living costs and limited opportunities for career advancement. Harvard Professors, Joseph Fuller and William Kerr, believe that the Great Resignation did not appear out of nowhere and there are five factors that changed the workforce—**retirement, relocation, reconsideration, reshuffling,** and **reluctance**. Going forward, their view is:

> Companies that have the vision and resources to offer flexibility to their employees are the most likely to maintain a stable and competitive workforce. And the companies best able to attract and retain talent will be those offering benefits that address the changing needs of workers. Similarly, companies that demonstrate a commitment to improving their employees long-term career prospects by offering training and tuition reimbursements will garner greater loyalty and gain in stature with prospective employees. The Great Resignation was no anomaly; the forces underlying it are here to stay.[15]

---

[15] Joseph Fuller and William Kerr. 'The Great Resignation Didn't Start with the Pandemic'. *Harvard Business Review*. March 2023. https://hbr.org/2022/03/the-great-resignation-didnt-start-with-the-pandemic

Hire Women at All Levels, for Different Roles

'Women with different backgrounds (such as in sales) can contribute a lot to your company and grow into successful technology leaders.'[16]

—Boston Consulting Group (BCG)

Employing women at all levels of an organization can boost productivity, company culture, as well as the company's financial performance. BlackRock's data shows that typically more women work in clerical roles and fewer work in senior and managerial roles.[17] But firms with workforce diversity at all levels outperformed less diverse companies by an average of 1.2 per cent between 2011 and 2022.[18] Organizations in Europe and North America outperformed the most by 2.1 per cent and 1.5 per cent respectively. Women at the top naturally change company culture. They have been known to promote the right female talent in key positions. Further, having several women in senior roles often correlates with a higher rate of women across the company.[19]

Companies are recommended to build the female talent pipeline. Consultancy firm, Boston Consulting Group recommends that in addition to setting up structured programmes, companies should work to expand their talent pool by looking

---

[16] Vaishali Rastogi, Michael Meyer, Michael Tan, and Justine Tasiaux. 'Boosting Women in Technology in Southeast Asia'. *Boston Consulting Group*. October 2020.

[17] Victoria Masterson. 'There's a sweet spot for gender diversity in the workplace, finds BlackRock – get it right and you'll outperform your peers'. *World Economic Forum*. November 2023.

[18] 'Lifting financial performance by investing in women'. *BlackRock*. November 2023.

[19] Vaishali Rastogi, Michael Meyer, Michael Tan, and Justine Tasiaux. 'Boosting Women in Technology in Southeast Asia'. *Boston Consulting Group*. October 2020.

beyond pure technology profiles, as some technical roles and skills can be built on top of other critical capabilities.[20] This is true, as we learned in the chapter on digital skills, as many women have indeed made this transition. In fact, when hiring for different roles, it can be useful to make a distinction between 'tech-lite' jobs and 'tech-heavy jobs', with both being just as valuable in different sectors of the digital economy. Tech-lite job roles, such as marketing executives, data analysts and sales executives, require skills that enable businesses to respond quickly to market changes and customer needs. These jobs have skills with a high degree of transferability. Tech-heavy job roles, such as software engineers and data engineers, are high in demand for businesses to leverage data and technology to deliver personalized and relevant customer experiences. In the long term, BCG recommends that companies carry out outreach to young girls in order to encourage interest in technology at an early age. Dr Vicki Gardiner from Australia's Computer Society agrees and thinks that such jobs need to be rebranded to girls in high school. 'It's not just about the coder in a dark room. Technology careers actually span a huge diversity in roles.'[21]

Create Inclusive Workplaces

'Culture eats strategy for breakfast.'[22]
—Peter Drucker, management consultant and
university professor

No matter how great your business strategy is, your plan will fail without a company culture that encourages people to implement

---

[20] Ibid.

[21] Kathryn Lewis. 'Failure to boost women in tech could cost economy $11b over 20 years'. *The Canberra Times*. June 2021.

[22] Stephen Conmy. 'What does culture eats strategy for breakfast mean?' Corporate Governance Institute.

it. You can find this advice in all great business books. Good company culture is often confused with how the early technology companies designed their offices with beer fridges, foosball tables, and beanbags. Great company culture is when employees and their managers can deal with pressure and challenges and treat each other with respect and integrity. A gender inclusive workplace can enhance company culture and recruit and retain women in digital jobs.

You may be wandering what does a gender inclusive place look like. Women-friendly workspaces are often described as safe and secure, and include flexible facilities like on-site gyms, day-care, and breast-feeding rooms. Others describe it as providing relevant benefits like maternity leave. BlackRock quite rightly said that the extent of a 'women-friendly workplace culture' is hard to measure. Nonetheless, they tested to see if the length of average maternity leave taken could be a useful measure. BlackRock found that:

> Incorporating maternity leave data into an investment portfolio helps boost returns. By overweighting companies with longer maternity leaves taken and underweighting companies with shorter maternity leaves taken, a hypothetical portfolio has yielded an outstanding 1.07% annualized excess return over the benchmark portfolio (Russell 1000 Index).[23]

Gender inclusive workplaces have transparent company policies, pay scales, and promotion criteria to ensure fairness and accountability. For example, Cisco has developed frameworks and processes to enhance its transparency, as it states that:

> [it] has always been committed to paying our people fairly and equitably. We've recently built an innovative and inclusive framework that introduces powerful analytics to evaluate our

---

[23] 'Lifting financial performance by investing in women'. *BlackRock*. November 2023.

complex compensation system and its overall health. These innovations help build the trusted environment that drives the best teams, allows us to retain the best talent, and positions.[24]

Have a Targeted Approach to Recruit Women

'Saying "women just don't apply for these roles" is a cop-out—the responsibility for fixing that sits with the hiring organisation.'[25]

—Mivy James, digital transformation director,
BAE Systems Applied Intelligence

The way in which a job advertisement is written can have a huge impact on whether someone fills out an application or switches off completely. Words like 'analyse', 'leader', and 'expert' have been found to be very masculine-focused, whilst words such as 'support' and 'together' appeal to women more. An analysis of more than 7,500 job adverts, conducted by the hiring platform Applied, ran the wording of each advert through a gender score calculator, a tool which detects feminine words (such as together, collaborate, responsibility, and share) and masculine words (such as individual, challenging, and driven) was used to score the text accordingly. The report found that adverts using strong masculine language saw the number of female candidates applying for the role drop by up to 10 per cent, with less than half applying for those positions.[26] But, when employers reduced the occurrences of masculine words and replaced them with feminine or neutral words, the proportion of female applicants was estimated to increase by up to 54 per cent.

---

[24] 'Pay Parity at Cisco'. *Cisco*.

[25] 'How do we get more women in tech?' *BCS*. March 2022. https://www.bcs. org/articles-opinion-and-research/how-do-we-get-more-women-in-tech/

[26] Caitlin Powell. '"Masculine" language in job adverts deterring female candidates, research finds'. *People Management*. August 2021. https://www. peoplemanagement.co.uk/article/1743030/masculine-language-job-adverts-deterring-female-candidates

To attract more women, companies are recommended to advertise jobs highlighting benefits that would appeal to women like maternity policies, childcare vouchers, and of course, flexible and remote working. Companies should also increase the visibility of women on their company website. If women only see photos of men, they'll immediately think that they won't fit in at the company. Where the job is advertised is also an important consideration. Men and women look for jobs in different places. Men are more likely to look at job platforms like Indeed and Monster, while women tend to look for reviews and recommendations. MIT Sloan professor, Emilio J. Castilla, said, 'If the perception of an organisation is favourable but the gender diversity of applicants is still imbalanced, recruiters and hiring managers might consider trying to identify untapped talent pipelines, such as women's colleges or professional women's groups or associations.'[27] Harvard University professor, Frank Dobbin, said that his analysis on corporate diversity programmes found that, 'any kind of recruitment that targets women has a huge effect on not just who comes through the door but also the numbers of women in management five or ten years later.'[28] Another strategy is to introduce employee referral programmes at all levels of an organization.

What Can Investors Do?

'We believe that young women are the early adopters of popular culture.'[29]

—Jeremy Liew, partner, Lightspeed Venture Partners

---

[27] Emilio J. Castilla and Hye Jin Rho. 'The Gendering of Job Postings in the Online Recruitment Process'. *MIT*. February 2023. https://mitsloan.mit.edu/ideas-made-to-matter/altering-gendered-language-job-postings-doesnt-help-attract-more-women

[28] Ibid.

[29] Riva Richmond. 'Meet The Men Who Invest In Women Entrepreneurs.' *Forbes*. August 2017.

There is a missed opportunity for investors to invest in female digital entrepreneurs. The scale of this missed opportunity was highlighted in Chapter three. However, some investors have been quick to spot a good investment when they see one. Adam Quinton, CEO of Lucas Point Ventures, invests heavily in female -founded or women-led companies. While there is a push to increase the number of female investors, who have been more willing to support female founders, immediate change can happen if current male investors, that make up the majority, rethink their investments. Quinton says that by investing in women, his failure rate is lower than average.[30] Kevin O'Leary, the *Shark Tank* investor known as 'Mr Wonderful', also invests in women-run businesses. 'I don't want to start gender warfare, because, frankly, I'd give money to a goat if I could get a return. [but] . . . not some of my returns, all of my returns, have come from the ones run by women or owned by women.'[31] What we learn from these men is that investors should look for companies with female representations, expand their networks, and share knowledge and resources.

Look For Companies with Female Representation and/or Gender Initiatives

'Investors value gender diversity, that's for sure.'[32]
        —Professor Thomas Lys, Kellog School of Management

As noted in our chapter on missed opportunities, investing in female entrepreneurs would generate higher returns for society as a whole, as women invest more of their income in their families compared

---

[30] Riva Richmond. 'Meet The Men Who Invest in Women Entrepreneurs'. *Forbes*. August 2017. https://www.forbes.com/sites/thestoryexchange/2017/08/09/meet-the-men-who-invest-in-women-entrepreneurs/

[31] Ibid.

[32] 'Yes, Investors Care About Gender Diversity'. *Kellogg Insight*. March 2020.

to men. Investors can tap into those returns and even give them a boost by adopting 'Gender Lens Investing' (GLI). The investment firm Goldman Sachs, for example, announced their global initiative 10,000 Women to provide practical education, mentoring, networking, and access to capital for women entrepreneurs.[33] GLI is an investment strategy to intentionally direct capital towards solutions that drive gender equality.[34] Applying this strategy means a robust and structured approach to looking for companies with female representation that makes a difference. For instance, at the investment selection stage, gender lens investors would evaluate the target companies' gender diversity in leadership, workplace policies that support women, and products or services that benefit women, such as access to finance, education, or healthcare for women and girls. At the terms and conditions stage, gender lens investors would require commitments from management around gender best practices and gender disaggregated reporting for accountability. These best practices and supporting data would be tracked during the investment cycle.

Expand your Network and Forge Partnerships

'If you're an investor, you can use directories such as Crunchbase and PitchBook to search for companies with female founders. Ask women you already talk with to refer you to other women.'[35]

—Alison Barr Allen, co-founder and
chief operating officer, Fast

---

[33] 'Empowering Women: 10,000 Women'. *Goldman Sachs.*

[34] Charvi Gangwani. 'Gender Lens Investing: Driving Financial Returns and Social Impact'. *Women's World Banking.* July 2023.

[35] Allison Barr Allen. 'Here Are Three Things You Can Do Right Now To Increase The Number Of Women In Tech'. *Forbes.* May 2021. https://www.forbes.com/sites/forbestechcouncil/2021/05/07/here-are-three-things-you-can-do-right-now-to-increase-the-number-of-women-in-tech/

Don't just wait for women-led start-ups to come to you—go out and find them! This is the advice that females are giving to male investors. This is exactly what a group of male investors in the Philippines set out to do. Manila Angel Investing Network (MAIN) was established by a small group of male corporate leaders and investors in 2016. GLI was not on its agenda.[36] The small group would meet in private social clubs, which were traditionally male spaces. The network focused mainly on the technology sector. While being open to female members, it was not a priority to intentionally recruit women to their network.

> Members don't know women, so basing on this referral process is challenging . . . We know there are powerful women in the Philippines, but the circle of our membership base is mostly male dominated; so most likely the people they will refer to us will most likely be more men than females.[37]

Over time MAIN evolved and embraced GLI in fourteen start-ups, four of which are women-led. They also entered into partnerships with women's groups, like Investing in Women, which increased angel investments into women-led SMEs in the Philippines. A female member who was uncomfortable at first due to the lack of women in MAIN said that the network has been transformed. She noted MAIN's commitment to appeal to women, citing the change in venue, the increasing formalization of events, and the explicit invitations for women to join quarterly pitch meetings as notable efforts.

---

[36] 'Investor's journey in Gender Lens Investing. Examples from the field'. *Investing in Women Asia*. June 2021.

[37] Ibid.

What Can Government Do?

'Male politicians co-operation on gender issues is very important.'[38]

—Mariana Duarte, gender program officer,
Inter-Parliamentary Union

Countries that are focused on growing their digital economies and digital talent should consider increasing female representation, which can lead to a meaningful increase in the country's GDP.[39] For instance, in Ireland, legislative reforms around equality and technology contributed to a jump in the percentage of women working over the past thirty years. At the same time, real GDP per person almost tripled in Ireland. The Irish example along with examples from Chile and Germany suggest that increasing the number of women working by ten percentage points could yield approximately a 5 per cent increase in economic output.[40]

There is an opportunity for government through ministries and regional and local government to implement digital policies that will protect women online, increase their digital literacy, and provide access to resources for digital entrepreneurship. Such policies could be part of wider gender equality or digital policies. Other policies could be targeted specifically for women and girls or for both men and women. Men must be part of the revolution and the government must also support men.

---

[38] Alice French, Rurika Imahashi, and Wataru Suzuki. 'Inside Japan's gender problem: The men tasked with empowering women'. *Nikkei Asia.* January 2023.

[39] 'Lifting global growth by investing in women. Long-term capitalism at BlackRock'. *Blackrock.* 2023.

[40] Ibid.

Support Men

'Try not to become a man of success, but rather try to become
a man of value.'

—Albert Einstein

As the role of men in our economy and society changes, it is essential
that the government supports them on this journey. *Research for the
State of the World's Fathers 2023* shows that, despite many men taking on
more caring responsibilities during the pandemic, too few workplaces
support men's well-being.[41] In addition, too few policies and
politicians even consider men's caregiving, and too few boys
grow up seeing it displayed by their own fathers.[42] However,
to support women participate and work in the digital economy
requires men to have the same support for balancing work and
family commitments. These include paternity leave policies that
allow fathers to take time off work to bond with their newborns
or help their partners during the early stages of parenting, and
policies around flexible work arrangements and men's health like
mental health support, fitness initiatives, and access to health
screenings. In 1974, Sweden was the first country in the world
to replace gender-specific maternity leave with gender-neutral
parental leave. A government policy that supports working
parents with the same rights and obligations for both women and
men makes it easier for parents in Sweden to find a decent work–
life balance. Interestingly, today Sweden ranks well in terms of
human capital. It has widespread use of digital technologies and
the general population has a high degree of basic digital skills.[43]

---

[41] Charlotte Edmond. 'Can a new chores app encourage men to do more housework
and help close the gender gap?' *World Economic Forum.* August 2023. https://www.
weforum.org/agenda/2023/08/housework-men-women-gender-gap-equality/

[42] 'State of the World's Fathers 2023'. *Equimundo.* https://www.equimundo.
org/resources/state-of-the-worlds-fathers-2023/

[43] Lidija Kralj. 'Sweden: a snapshot of digital skills'. *Digital Skills and Jobs Platform.
European Union.* June 2023.

Promote Digital Skills

'If we do not promote the fair and full participation of girls and women in the digital future of our societies, we are setting ourselves up for a digital future that will be less rich, less innovative and less fair.'[44]

—Ulrik Knudsen, deputy secretary-general, OECD

Belgium has extensive policy experience in gender equality. Since the 1980s, it has implemented legal measures to promote gender equality and equal opportunities at the federal and regional levels, in both the public and private sectors. In terms of the digital economy, it has implemented a five year national plan 'Women in Digital 2021-2026', which is coordinated by the Ministry of the Economy Belgium.[45] One of the strategies is to turn digital skills into an everyday reality and to prepare teenage girls for a digitalized world.[46] Some of the key actions involve organizing information sessions in schools about future jobs and the skills needed for them, explaining basic computer science, and ensuring that everyone masters (soft) skills needed and improving training material for teachers.

Belgium is not alone in its efforts to boost digitals skills among women. There are examples from every continent. But more action at country and local level of government is required. Policymakers should strive to create a strategy that outlines basic, intermediate, and advanced levels of digital skills required by individuals. Governments and schools play a critical role in this goal. A technology curriculum needs to start as early as possible,

---

[44] 'What are the effects of AI on the Working Lives of Women?' UNESCO. March 2022

[45] 'Belgium - The national and intersectoral strategy "Women in Digital 2021-2026"'. *Digital Skills and Jobs Platform.* https://digital-skills-jobs.europa.eu/en/actions/national-initiatives/national-strategies/belgium-national-and-intersectoral-strategy-women

[46] Women in Digital: National and Intersectoral Strategy'. *BeDigitalTogether.*

and the environment needs to be attractive and conducive for both male and female students.

Women already in the workforce should also have access to additional training, and the government can provide this. To further women's careers in the digital economy, Belgium's masterplan encourages reskilling. 'In reality, women could be face[d] with specific barriers when they want to reskill themselves, master the necessary skills or follow training in a new field of expertise (artificial intelligence, etc.). They need to be supported when trying to adapt to technological changes that impact the job market.'[47] It recommends work placements or training and courses that allow women to gain their first experience in the digital sector and paying extra attention to women who are out of work on unemployment benefits. Belgium's experience is that:[48]

> Women in vulnerable groups are less likely to have access to information, training and jobs in the digital sector, but when we involve and encourage them, they are equally capable of mastering new digital skills and steering their career towards the digital sector.

Support Female Digital Businesses

> 'This programme is not only for the basic digital entrepreneurship but also insights to be able to compete in the national market and scale-up in the international market to financial literacy and cyber security.'[49]

> —Johnny G. Plate, minister of
> communication and information, Indonesia

---

[47] 'Women in Digital: National and Intersectoral Strategy'. *BeDigitalTogether*.

[48] Ibid.

[49] 'Indonesian Women Entrepreneurs Boost Digital Technology'. *OpenGov Asia*. https://opengovasia.com/indonesian-women-entrepreneurs-boost-digital-technology/

The Indonesian government wants to be an innovative and digital powerhouse and has been building a robust digital framework to meet this vision. Part of the framework involves supporting digital businesses and women which contribute to 60 per cent of the total MSMEs in Indonesia. However, women tend to face challenges, specifically in terms of business networking and marketing skills. The Communication and Information Minister urged industry stakeholders involved in the nation's digital ecosystem to provide training and skills development for women. 'Let us support modern Kartinis to migrate as well as Indonesians to enter the digital space for the prosperity of the nation and the people together.'[50] The Indonesian government is providing opportunities for women by establishing the Digital Entrepreneurship Academy, which includes a special programme designed for housewives to train and be digital-based entrepreneurs.[51] The government has also launched several wider initiatives to facilitate warungs digitalize. In 2023, the government signed a partnership with private sector players as part of a new Digital Technology Adoption Program 4.0 that provides digital mentoring and business incubation facilities to improve business capabilities.[52] By partnering with industry, the government can build strong women's networks and ensure that best practices are leveraged across all technology sectors. Indonesian female entrepreneurs stand to gain from this programme as the

[50] 'Digital transformation encourages women's equality in business'. *Antara News*. April 2022. https://en.antaranews.com/news/226145/digital-transformation-encourages-womens-equality-in-business-govt

[51] 'Indonesian Women Entrepreneurs Boost Digital Technology'. *OpenGov Asia*. May 2022. https://opengovasia.com/indonesian-women-entrepreneurs-boost-digital-technology/

[52] 'Partnering with SIRCLO, Ministry of Communication and Information Launches Digital Technology Adoption 4.0 & MSME Business Incubation'. *Indonesia Sentinel*. May 2023. https://indonesiasentinel.com/2023/05/29/partnering-with-sirclo-kominfo-launches-digital-technology-adoption-4-0-msme-business-incubation/

government knows that the economic contribution of women in the country is significant. If revenues of female-owned businesses increased to those comparable to male-owned firms, Indonesia's economy could unlock more than $428 million annually.[53] If the female labour force participation rate increased to 58 per cent, which is Indonesia's G20 commitment, GDP growth could increase by 0.7 per cent and add $62 billion to the economy.[54]

There are many examples of warungs in other countries. There are *sari-sari* stores in the Philippines, the *kirana* store in India, and villages shops in the UK. Regardless of size and location, government can help women overcome the challenges of establishing and scaling successful digital businesses. Targeted government programmes can provide resources, funding, and mentorship like access to business advisory services, legal support, and marketing assistance. Financial support can be part of wider stimulus packages in government budgets, as well as programmes that facilitate networking and access to global markets and expertise.

Measure Women's Contributions

'No industry or country can reach its full potential until women reach their full potential. This is especially true of science and technology, where women with a surplus of talent still face a deficit of opportunity.'[55]

—Sheryl Sandberg, former chief operating officer, Meta

---

[53] Marie Christine Apedo amah, Jescinta Isimeme Izevbigie, Alexandre Lauresalman Alibhai. 'It takes a village: Public-Private partnerships to foster Indonesian women's economic participation'. *World Bank*. June 2023. https://blogs.worldbank.org/developmenttalk/it-takes-village-public-private-partnerships-foster-indonesian-womens-economic

[54] 'Economic Gains from Investing in Childcare: The Case of Indonesia'. *World Bank Group*. January 2023. https://documents.worldbank.org/en/publication/documents-reports/documentdetail/099110010032227938/p1721820ecba5d0e90ad6206b56b8a2986e

[55] 'Sheryl Sandberg joins global women leaders in tech to demand gender equality'. *Barefoot College International*. January 2015.

Defining the digital economy is just the first step. To understand real impact, challenges, and opportunities requires a targeted approach. That needs numbers. But not just any numbers. Robust and consistent numbers. Throughout the chapters, evidence based on data has been provided where available. But it is patchy. Countries and businesses don't always measure the same things. There are two approaches to measuring the digital economy that could be taken. The first is a 'bottom-up' approach, which considers the digital economy to be a 'limited' set of economic activities that produce ICT goods and digital services that facilitate the digitalization of the economy.[56] The second, is a 'top-down' approach in which the digital economy includes 'any' economic activity enabled by the use of ICT goods and digital services. The second approach reflects the extent of digitalization in the economy and is the one that the international organizations are attempting to measure. It's a mammoth task and one that includes collecting data on digital products, as well as the production and consumption of non-digital products that are obtained through digital means, whether digitally ordered, digitally delivered, or both. Organizations like UN Trade and Development and OECD, and governments, are tackling this task as the benefits outweigh the costs.

As the measurement of the digital economy becomes well established it would be important to extend the analysis to measure the contribution from women and girls and, later on, to other minority and vulnerable groups. To date, there is no exact measure of women's digital contribution but all data points in the same direction—the figure is significant, but it could be more. Developing metrics to understand the evolving role of women in the digital economy can identify areas where further

---

[56] *Handbook on Measuring Digital Trade.* The International Monetary Fund, the Organisation for Economic Co-operation and Development, the United Nations and the World Trade Organization. 2023. https://www.elibrary.imf.org/display/book/9789287073600/CH008.xml

support and opportunities are needed to promote gender diversity and inclusion. An iterative process would serve well as the digital economy continues to grow and change how we work, play, connect, live, and learn.

> What can companies, investors, and governments do to ride the revolution?

> Different digital economic agents must take action. Companies can offer flexible and remote work to women (and men). They can hire women at all levels for different roles, create inclusive workplaces, and have a targeted approach to hiring women. At the same time, investors can look to invest in companies with female representation/gender initiatives and can expand their networks to include women. Finally, government must also play a key role. Governments must support men as their role in our economy and society changes. They must also support women in developing digital skills and setting up digital businesses. Lastly, government must attempt to measure women's contribution, however difficult it may be, in recognition of its importance to provide tailored solutions to the challenges.

The Female Digital Revolution

'A radical and pervasive change in society and the social structure.'[1]

—Definition of revolution, Collins Dictionary

The Ancient Greek philosopher Heraclitus observed that the natural world was in a constant state of movement. People age, develop habits, and move environments. Technology will change too and there is already talk of what future revolutions will look like. For example, in the sixth industrial revolution, it is predicted that quantum computing and nanotechnology will change our economies and societies. Some countries are already planning for future technological advancements. Germany is investing in AI, robotics, and sustainable technologies, and South Korea is developing smart cities. In this world of change, our digital societies are evolving and humanity must be nurtured. However, there is less talk on the future of the female revolution, the accomplishments women have made so far, and how our digital economies can be more inclusive in the future. From a gender perspective, there are some estimates that the pandemic has taken us backwards. The World Economic Forum reported that closing global gender gaps in economic participation and opportunity will take 169 years, which is up from the pre-pandemic period.[2]

---

[1] Collins English Dictionary.

[2] 'The Global Gender Gap Report 2023'. *World Economic Forum*. 2023.

To forge a brighter future, we must take stock, reflect, and learn from the past. We did this at the start of the journey, where we sought to understand the different industrial revolutions and how digitalization is driving our economies to rapidly expand. We also studied the changing role of women during the decades of industrial revolution. Drawing on the economic insights of Professor Claudia Goldin, we found how women's aspirations for their future has changed, altering their life choices and career paths. When we understand these two drivers, we understand the female digital revolution. Some of this revolution is in the media spotlight, for example, in women who are celebrities or hold positions of political power that are solving real-world problems. It can also be witnessed in reading stories about Lisa Su, the Taiwanese lady heading the global semiconductor company in the AI chip competition war; Vrinda Gupta, the woman setting up her own credit card when she was rejected for one; Dr Lisa Dyson, the woman developing air protein to enhance food security; and Dr Claire Novorol, the female doctor helping you track health symptoms and find the right doctor. Some aspects of the revolution remain unnoticed and can be found in changemakers in our local communities, like female farmers learning to use drones to manage crops, women that teach cybersecurity in local schools, women-owned warungs in Indonesia using digital payments, or women creating digital libraries for children living in remote areas. It is not just AI and drones that are being adopted. Technology like robotics, blockchain, metaverse, and developments in quantum computing, driven by women like Professor Michelle Simmons, have the potential to provide women more benefits in how they work, play, learn, and manage their finances, health, home, and save the planet.

Women are not to be overlooked and be underestimated. Their purchasing power is increasing from $20 trillion worldwide every year, and events like the Women's Football World Cup show

how the economy can benefit. But there are challenges, and we explore the different missed opportunities and how significant they can be. For instance, there is a target for women to obtain equal access to the internet by 2030.[3] Missing this target would delay all the benefits that the internet provides, like opportunities to start new businesses, sell products in new markets, and find better-paid jobs and careers, learn, and have access to quality healthcare and financial services. Men are part of the solution, and we must also understand their own challenges.

Different policy levers at international, government, and company level are needed to ride the female digital revolution. The Belgium government has developed a national plan to support women in the digital government, and the Japanese government is trying to 'shake off' its male dominated culture. India is teaching future entrepreneurs to tinker, and investors in Philippines made their angel investing network more inclusive to women. Companies are making it easier for women (and men) to manage work–life balance and are proud when female representation in their companies is visible.

Role models with different backgrounds like Taylor Swift, Dr Fei-Fei Li, Christina Junqueira, and Professor Claudia Goldin—to name a few—can provide valuable lessons in educating and inspiring future generations that risk missing out and being future role models. Women, no matter what profession you are in or aspiring to be in, you can be part of the digital economy. Whether you are a lawyer, accountant, marketing professional, or even a nurse, you will need to learn how to use digital technologies in some way. Get ahead. Let us learn and be ready for the next digital revolution.

---

[3] "In 2022, ITU developed a framework in conjunction with the Office of the Secretary-General's Envoy on Technology (OSET), which includes a target on gender parity in Internet access to be met by 2030". 'Bridging the gender divide'. *ITU*. November 2023.

Acknowledgements

The idea for the book was cooking in my head for a long time. So, I am grateful for the team at Penguin Random House SEA for believing in this idea, making it a reality, and publishing this book. Thank you for supporting me in this process.

I would like to express my sincere gratitude to the women and men celebrated in this book. Without you, there would be no female digital revolution, and there would be no story to tell. Thank you to all the people who generously agreed to be interviewed. I appreciate your stories, insights, and expertise that shaped my research.

I also want to acknowledge the organizations, institutions, and communities dedicated to advancing gender diversity and inclusion in the digital economy. Many of them have been mentioned in this book. Your work is vital, and I am proud to be a part of this collective effort for positive change.

A heartfelt thanks to my mentors and peers in the fields of economics, law, business, leadership, and technology for their support in creating this book. Thank you for reading and commenting on drafts, reviewing book cover designs, and providing honest and valuable feedback.

Special thanks to my family and friends (near and far) for cheering me on every step of the way. Writing this book has been both a vulnerable and empowering journey. I am lucky to have you in my life.

Lastly, I would like to thank you for reading this book.

www.ingramcontent.com/pod-product-compliance
Lightning Source LLC
Chambersburg PA
CBHW030511210326
41597CB00013B/866